From SOCIALISM to MARKET ECONOMY

The Transition Problem

William S. Kern, Editor

1992

W.E. UPJOHN INSTITUTE for Employment Research
Kalamazoo, Michigan

Library of Congress Cataloging-in-Publication Data

From socialism to market economy : the transition problem / William S.
  Kern, editor.
     p.   cm.
  Includes bibliographical references and index.
  ISBN 0-88099-129-1 (hard). — ISBN 0-88099-130-5 (pbk.)
     1. Soviet Union—Economic policy—1986-1991—Congresses.   2. Post-
  communism—Soviet Union—Congresses.   3. Europe, Eastern—Economic
  policy—1989—Congresses.   4. Post-communism—Europe, Eastern—
  Congresses.   I. Kern, William S., 1952-
  HC336.26.F77   1992
  338.947—dc2   92-26336
                                                                        CIP

THE INSTITUTE, a nonprofit research organization, was established on July 1, 1945.
It is an activity of the W.E. Upjohn Unemployment Trustee Corporation, which was
formed in 1932 to administer a fund set aside by the late Dr. W.E. Upjohn for the purpose of carrying on "research into the causes and effects of unemployment and measures for the alleviation of unemployment."

The facts presented in this study and the observations and viewpoints expressed are the
sole responsibility of the authors. They do not necessarily represent positions of the
W.E. Upjohn Institute for Employment Research.

Cover design by J.R. Underhill.
Index prepared by Shirley Kessel.
Printed in the United States of America.

ACKNOWLEDGMENTS

The papers in this volume were presented during the twenty-seventh Annual Lecture-Seminar Series conducted by the Department of Economics at Western Michigan University during the 1990-91 school year. The series is made possible through the generous financial support of the W.E. Upjohn Institute for Employment Research and the College of Arts and Sciences of Western Michigan University. I wish to express my gratitude to my colleagues in the Department of Economics for their helpful support and encouragement, especially the members of the Lecture Series Committee including Wei-Chiao Huang and Mike Ross.

William S. Kern

Kalamazoo, Michigan
July 1992

iii

CONTENTS

Introduction

William S. Kern
Western Michigan University

With stunning speed the socialist experiments of Eastern Europe and the Soviet Union have now apparently come to an end. Despite half a century or more of efforts directed by Communist leaders toward building socialism, the citizens of these countries now find that the structure for which they had endured great sacrifices will not survive. The citizens of these nations are now faced with the prospect of constructing a new economic structure based upon a foundation of markets and private ownership.

The problems produced by the transformation of these economies was the theme of a lecture series held at Western Michigan University during the 1990-91 school year. The lectures presented form the basis of this volume.

The volume begins with Paul Marer's paper, which examines the major obstacles in the path of countries seeking to convert their economies to market systems. It serves as a natural starting point, as it provides an excellent overview of the major issues to be faced by the countries in the process of transition.

Marer points out that the countries of Eastern Europe have several models to emulate in creating their own market economies. These options include a social market economy of the sort typified by West Germany or a consumerist market economy of the U.S. type. The third model is a Japanese-style corporatist economy. Marer's opinion is that the East European nations are most likely to emulate the first of these versions. A social market economy fits more closely the cultural attitudes and social vision of these peoples than with the other models.

Marer argues that all successful market systems of whatever type exhibit a common set of institutional traits that are the source of their success. These include private ownership of the means of production, the presence of strong competition and freedom of trade, a strong and convertible currency, an efficient system of financial intermediation, avoidance of prohibitive taxation, adequate infrastructure including environmental protection, a pluralist and stable political system, and the freedom to pursue personal goals.

In contrast, Marer observes that the legacy of the socialist experiments of Eastern Europe and the USSR is devoid of almost all of these features that effective market systems require. Marer's essay, therefore, concentrates discussion upon matters of institutional change and the creation of new institutions as the primary focus of the transition process. His essay surveys the current state of affairs with regard to the above-mentioned institutional structure in the East European nations. In each case he describes the legacy of the previous system and the major obstacles facing institutional change, and he offers suggestions for various "transformation options"—the pros and cons of alternative transition strategies. The essay concludes with discussion of strategic issues such as timing and the speed of reforms and the potential role of western aid in the transition process.

The paper by Abram Bergson shifts the focus to consideration of economic reforms in the Soviet Union. Bergson's paper provides us with a sort of "report card" or progress report on reforms in the Gorbachev era in that it indicates the nature of the reforms initiated and examines the difficulties produced as a consequence of those efforts. Bergson begins by examining the pre-Gorbachev structure of the economy and its performance. He identifies the impetus to *perestroika* as stemming from recognition of increasing stagnation of the rate of economic growth relative to earlier periods and to that of the West.

Bergson points out that Gorbachev's initial response to these difficulties was to propose a restructuring of industrial planning which sought to substitute market forces for bureaucratic control in the area of enterprise operation. He reports that little actual change resulted from this attempt, a result which he attributes to the continued dominance of "state orders" in guiding production, bureaucratic opposition, lack of financial discipline, and the lack of a real price system.

Bergson also surveys the results of other elements of *perestroika* such as changes in property relations and the legalization of private enterprise. Here again Bergson indicates that the changes have met with rather limited success, though the growth of cooperatives appears to be an encouraging sign. Bergson identifies onerous taxation, ideological hostility, and the distortive effects of the material supply system and Soviet prices as primary obstacles to the growth of private enterprise.

Bergson devotes particular attention to the circumstances of the breakdown of the consumer goods market. He points out that while the consumer market has seldom worked well, its current status is nothing short of disastrous. The culprit Bergson identifies is a burgeoning government budget deficit which has pumped a considerable amount of purchasing power into a market already chronically in a state of excess demand. This has led to unfortunate side effects, including a "falling off of interest in work."

Bergson finds the lack of success of *perestroika* not too surprising, given the immensity of the task and the short period of time that has elapsed, though there is clearly an undercurrent of criticism by Bergson of the manner in which the reforms were instituted. One gets a sense that he feels "mismanagement" or lack of conceptual vision on the part of Gorbachev contributed to the current situation. He rather diplomatically asks "whether, with more skillful management at the highest level, a more favorable outcome might not have been achievable."

Joseph Berliner offers us a perspective on the origins on Gorbachev's reform efforts. Berliner's key insight is his characterization of *perestroika* as a "revolution from above." He reports that Soviet economic reforms, unlike those of Eastern Europe, stemmed originally not from a state of crisis or impending collapse, or even from widespread dissatisfaction of the common man. Rather, the impetus for reform arose initially from the "enlightened wing" of Communist leadership which was concerned primarily about the effects of long-term trends of lower growth rates and feeble technical progress.

The fact that *perestroika* was imposed from the top down rather than bubbling up from below explains, Berliner tells us, some of its characteristic features and peculiarities. Among those features, Berliner singles out three as being of particular importance. *Perestroika* has been actively opposed by a number of groups including workers and bureaucrats who felt threatened by the changes. Hence, *perestroika* has never had widespread popular support to invigorate it. A second effect has been a sort of aimless drift of the reform process. Those who initiated the reforms were members of a group that had never seriously questioned the overall effectiveness of the central planning mechanism and had therefore never considered alternatives to that basic framework. Last, Berliner identifies the rationale of *glasnost* and its connection to *perestroika* as arising from the same seed. He asserts that Gorbachev recognized that reforms that would need to be carried out by the party and the economic bureaucracy would be sabotaged; hence, these groups could not be counted upon to promote reform efforts. *Glasnost* thus was something of a propaganda campaign designed to discredit the existing system and its defenders and elicit popular support for reform.

Though Berliner's essay goes to considerable length to describe the disruption of the economy produced by *perestroika* and the political obstacles to solutions, one nonetheless is able to detect an occasional note of optimism in his assessment of the longer term possibilities. He sees the development of the cooperative movement and the emergence of entrepreneurial endeavors as hopeful signs of a "grass roots" movement that may be "the foundation for a subsequent major transformation of the economy."

While Bergson's and Berliner's essays seek to survey the overall impact of *perestroika*, Paul Gregory's paper narrows our focus to consideration of the role of an institution of key importance in this process—the Soviet economic bureaucracy.

Gregory characterizes *perestroika* as having proceeded in a series of stages or steps. The first stage comprising the first three to four years of Gorbachev's leadership was characterized by rather naive thinking on the part of Soviet leaders who thought that their long-term economic decline could be reversed by relatively minor reforms of the existing economic mechanism. The second stage, beginning about 1988-89, resulted from Gorbachev's recognition that the beliefs guiding reform in stage one were wrong. During stage two, Gorbachev sought to weaken bureaucratic control over the economy by a series of legislative actions as well as by a campaign designed to discredit bureaucrats. The third stage, which for a long time Gorbachev seemed to wish to hold in abeyance but which in light of recent events can no longer be prevented, includes the more radical reforms leading to a full-fledged market economy.

Gregory's paper deals primarily with the opposition to reform mounted during stage two by bureaucrats. He points out that bureaucrats, who exhibited a natural antipathy toward the reform movement because of its impact upon their power and prestige, mounted their own propaganda campaign which proposed to demonstrate that delay or avoidance of reforms was in the public interest. Gregory's discussions with bureaucrats reveal that their opposition stems from concerns not only about their own situation but also about the disruptive impacts of the reforms.

Gregory points out that bureaucratic arguments, while based upon relevant concerns—inflation will result, monopolies may arise, etc.—often fail to consider that the reforms will, in the long run, produce a more efficient system. In particular, Gregory finds fault with Soviet bureaucrats' reluctance to consider that policies might be instituted to deal with the unfortunate effects of reform. For instance, while the privatization of the economy might well lead to the creation of monopoly power, bureaucratic planners would "plan" for competition through the creation of additional firms by the state rather than developing antitrust law and fostering competition through removing barriers to entry. Many of the difficulties with bureaucratic arguments he traces to widespread misunderstanding of the role of prices and of market forces in general.

Gregory demonstrates that as a result of Gorbachev's efforts at discrediting the bureaucracy, much of the old command system has been broken down without its replacement by market institutions. The result has been an even more chaotic environment, and an unfortunate side-effect has been that the resulting chaos has been attributed to marketization reforms rather than to the collapse of the planning system.

Herbert Levine's essay on the transition process points out a unique feature of the socialist reform efforts—the lack of a theory or model of the transition process. Reformers in the socialist nations can observe the features of market economies which serve as something of a blueprint for their efforts, but they have little clear guidance about how to bring such institutional structures into existence in their own countries. The situation is akin to that of a person armed with a blueprint of a "dream home," but without any carpentry skills.

Levine argues that there are two factors of key importance in the transition process: the interrelatedness of the changes that have to be made and the requirement of simultaneity in their imposition. Levine points out that even simple changes in one aspect of the economy will require a mushrooming of changes in other areas to accommodate it. Levine cites the example of the desire to change the responsiveness of Soviet managers as a case in point. In order to change managers' behavior they must be given the power to make a whole range of decisions about the use of labor, materials, and machinery. But giving managers such power requires elimination of the system of central material supply, the creation of the right to hire and fire workers, and the right to select technologies and acquire capital, which in turn requires the creation of a banking system based on a new set of lending principles. The process requires an effective price system and macroeconomic stability as well, in order for these decisions to lead to desirable results.

Levine argues that for these reforms to be effective, they must take place more or less simultaneously. This is of course a result of the interrelatedness factor just discussed. Changes in one part of the economy are dependent on changes having been made elsewhere before they can proceed. Undertaking all of these changes simultaneously raises the probability of significant disequilibria occurring.

The final essay in the series, by Josef Brada, directs our attention toward the transition problems specific to the countries of Eastern Europe. Brada informs us that these countries are currently involved in three related processes. These include the long-run process of transforming the economy into some form of market system, the short-run process of eliminating the macroeconomic disturbances caused by the transition process, and the process of rejoining the world economy. Brada states that these three processes interact with one another "often in ways that seem unpredictable to policymakers and that are not clearly understood by the population." Brada surveys each of these processes indicating the major conceptual issues and problems arising in each of these areas. He examines the specifics of the cases of Hungary, Czechoslovakia, and Poland.

A major theme of Brada's paper is the limited window of opportunity available to political leaders in dealing with the range of problems that the transition process has thrust upon them. After years of listening to the unfulfilled promises of their Communist leaders, they are now impatient and unlikely to rally to leaders who promise a better future at the cost of still more current sacrifice. Indeed, this may be the toughest problem of all faced by the countries involved in this process.

As noted in the beginning of this introduction, these essays are based on lectures presented over the course of the 1990-91 school year. Obviously, tremendous changes have taken place in the former Soviet Union during the interim between the writing of the papers and their appearance here in print. The essays continue to inform, however, as they illuminate factors at work in the past and identify still unresolved issues. They reflect the opinions of some of the most knowledgeable of analysts of the Soviet economy at a particular point in time, and provide a backdrop for developments as they continue to unfold. I believe they will continue to provide us with valuable insights about the process of economic reform in these nations and add to the historical record of that period in the reform process.

Roadblocks to Changing Economic Systems in Eastern Europe

Paul Marer
Indiana University

Paper presented
September 19, 1990

The eight "socialist" or former socialist countries of Central, Eastern, and Southern Europe can be divided into two groups of four nations: those in which the body politic has made a *seemingly* firm commitment to become a market economy (the German Democratic Republic, Czechoslovakia, Hungary, and Poland); and those in which the body politic has not (or not yet) made such a commitment and still believes that some kind of a third way of "market socialism," a system that combines central planning and the market, is feasible (Bulgaria, Romania, Yugoslavia, and Albania). To be sure, Yugoslavia is difficult to classify since Slovenia and Croatia have a strong preference to join the first group, but the other republics are not willing to go along with their choice. The USSR would belong to the second group, although there too not all republics see eye-to-eye on this issue.

This essay is about the nature and problems of the transition faced by the countries that appear to have made a commitment to become full-fledged market economies. (Why their commitment is dubbed "apparent" will be explained later.) The next section identifies the three main models of successful market economies. It is important for those of us in the West who wish to advise policymakers in Central and Eastern Europe on transition to a market economy, and for policymakers in those countries working on transition problems who wish to learn from the experiences of successful market economies to recognize that in different historical, social, political, cultural, and economic environments, alternative institutional arrangements and policies can be successful. This suggests caution in seeking to duplicate some particular feature of another country's economic system.

After focusing on the differences between market economy systems, the essay identifies and discusses briefly those system features and causal relationships that successful market economies appear to have in common. Assuming that the factors identified are the right ones, I venture the hypothesis that successful transition programs in Central and Eastern Europe will be those that can duplicate just those system features and policies that seem to account for the successes among the market economy countries, irrespective of the economic, social, cultural, and political differences among them.

Next, I examine the economic legacies inherited by the new governments in Central and Eastern Europe, following the framework presented in the previous section. The purpose is to try to identify the nature and size of the gap between what is and what should be, a gap that transition programs should attempt to close. On each set of issues I discuss the main policy options and make recommendations.

The concluding part of the essay offers some thoughts on the strategy of transition, calls attention to the immense intellectual, economic, and political difficulties of transition, and speculates about policy implications for the United States and the West.

Models of Successful Market Economies

As I see it, there are three main models of successful market economies: the West European social market economy, the U.S. consumer market economy, and the Japanese corporatist market economy. Let me describe briefly the main differences among them.[1]

Although there are vast differences even among the countries of Western Europe, the successful European paradigm is best exemplified by the *social market economy* of Germany. There is an unquestioned commitment to the predominance of market forces and of private property; "social market" simply means a recognition that an unbridled market has imperfections and that it is the state's responsibility to rectify them. The state is responsible for sound monetary and fiscal policies (a task that successive German governments have met in particularly exemplary fashion), allowing relatively free foreign competition on the domestic market (with agriculture being the most notable exception); efficient infrastructure, some attention to the environment; adequate health care, education, and the right of just about all citizens to decent (which in some cases means subsidized) housing; job security for the large majority of the workforce (that has parallels with the U.S. Civil Service); and substantial government programs to help the unemployed and the poor.

The basic idea of a social market economy is making capitalism more humane in order to sustain political support for the system, but not to interfere with market forces so much as to lose the efficiency gains of capitalism. The line between what the private sector provides via the interplay of market forces and what the state provides as a matter of political right is, to some extent, blurred. Germany's economic performance (as well as that of the other West European countries) has been helped by the willingness of its people to save and to work hard, traits that to a degree are culturally determined.

In Germany, as in the other countries of (especially Northern) Europe, the social and business infrastructures are excellent, the cities are generally more livable than those in the United States, and there exists only a relatively small underclass of "have not" persons. But it should not be forgotten that these achievements came relatively recently, not early in the period of postwar reconstruction and expansion. Behind the success is decades of painful sacrifice, initially including high unemployment. Furthermore, Europe's property rights under the current system are much less entrepreneurial and adaptive than property rights under the U.S. system. The most revealing evidence for this is their highly disparate rates of growth in long-term job creation. To be sure, Europe's problems are being addressed by the 1992 process of economic integration, which borrows some of the best features of the American system.

As an aside, note that the difference between a German-type social market economy and the "market socialism" ideas in Eastern Europe and the Soviet Union is fundamental. Although there is no precise or fully agreed to definition of market socialism, its advocates believe that the introduction of *limited* market forces can help preserve an economic system in which the means of production should remain predominantly nonprivate, the government should play a substantial role in directing economic activities, and the distribution of income and wealth should be relatively egalitarian. Market socialism often entails giving workers a substantial role in management. Advocates of market socialism are suspicious, often for ideological reasons, of capitalism and of markets; market socialism is their terminal of retreat in the face of the proven basic faults of a centrally planned economic system.[2]

The U.S. model, termed a *consumer market economy*, assigns a powerful role to the pull and push market forces (and only a minor role to the government) to promote economic growth through adaptation. The entrepreneurial spirit is vigorous and the mobility of the factors of production, including labor, is high. The efficiency of the market is praised and government interference is criticized (although reality is not as extreme as the image). To be sure, long-run market efficiency is probably impaired by the often short-term horizons of corporations, the get-rich-quick schemes chased by many entrepreneurs, and by the inordinate amount of litigation and financial manipulation that are also a part of the system. Government regulation (and deregulation) typically targets as the beneficiary the consumer rather than the producer. Social pressures and government policies promote private consumption over saving. This preference is reflected not only in individual and corporate behavior but sometimes also in irresponsibly large deficits in the government budget.

Critics note that the U.S. paradigm excessively promotes the virtues of short-term market efficiency and individual consumption over long-term growth, equity, and addressing social problems. There is an underprovision of social investment. America's infrastructure has been deteriorating. And a large underclass, with no stake in the prevailing economic and social order, has emerged and is being perpetuated.

Japan's paradigm, termed a *corporatist market economy*, is a particularly successful blend of features rooted in Japan's own environment and traditions.[3] One of its main features is intense competition for greater market shares rather than for short-term profits. This has led to long-term thinking and continuous improvements in efficiency, productivity, and cost-competitiveness, even though the domestic market has been sheltered—often for long periods, until domestic firms in an industry have matured fully—from foreign competition. Most Japanese firms have a strong commitment to employment security, but not to the preservation of the specific jobs of individual workers. This, in turn, has justified large corporate expenditures on retraining programs and relocation. Together with Japan's rapid rate of growth and the downward flexibility of wages, these features have contributed to its enviable record of full employment, flexible market adaptation, and spectacular economic success.

Perhaps no factor is more important in the Japanese model than its promotion of an extraordinarily high level of voluntary savings and investment. These are prompted by the pressures as well as opportunities of its economic system, by its government's policies (providing large incentives to save and a stable financial framework), as well as by the traditions of the Japanese culture. There is a close working relationship between the government on the one hand and business and labor unions on the other. The bureaucracy has maintained and uses skillfully its authority over the private sector, mostly by assisting producers rather than consumers or labor.

We should not forget that Japan's spectacular success is of relatively recent fruition; in the later 1950s, its level of development was measured to be on par with those of the USSR and the countries of Eastern Europe, on average. Japan has achieved what it has today by sacrificing consumption over a long period; by working extremely hard, including the sacrifice of leisure (an attitude that is instilled in early childhood); and to some extent also by neglecting a bit its infrastructure, the environment, and (until recently) the global burdens shouldered by other large and economically successful nations.

The newly industrialized countries of Asia (e.g., Korea, Taiwan, Hong Kong, and Singapore) have much in common with Japan's paradigm, although no two countries have fully identical economic policies and systems.

Common Causal Factors
in Successful Market Economies

Although there are major variations in the economic systems and policies among even the successful capitalist market economies, the economic systems and policies of such countries appear to have shared, to a greater or lesser degree, the following essential features.

1. *Private Ownership*. The means of production are predominantly privately owned. State-owned enterprises, in some cases accounting for as much as one-third or more of output, have played a more important role during the early stages of reconstruction and development, when unemployment was still high and voluntary savings still low, than subsequently. State enterprises tend to be more efficient when they function in a competitive environment than when they are insulated. In a competitive environment, state ownership does not automatically mean gross inefficiency if the firms receive no subsidies or the subsidies are given in ways that do not cancel the pressures and rewards of market forces for the firm. However, since the operation of state-owned firms is difficult to insulate from political and bureaucratic pressures, practically all the industrial countries have implemented programs of privatization in recent years.

2. *Competition and Trade*. The single most important feature of a well-functioning market system is strong competition. Countries whose domestic markets are large enough to accommodate more than a handful of firms in each industry, such as Japan, could afford to be protectionist and still maintain strong competition. However, countries that are small or medium-sized must open up to import competition

and eventually direct foreign investment. Full competition requires sound and predictable rules and regulations in all areas of production and trade. It is the government's responsibility to establish and enforce them, unless industry or trade associations can do the job as well or better.

3. *Sound Currency.* One of the essential functions of government is to provide a sound currency. This means a low rate of inflation and full convertibility as soon as practicable. The rate of inflation can be kept manageable only with sound monetary and fiscal policies (for which there are general guidelines but no precise recipes); the same is also a precondition for meaningful convertibility. A low rate of inflation and the expectation that inflation will not get out of hand are necessary to motivate business firms—as well as households as savers and providers of labor services—to take the long view and to focus on real economic activities instead of devoting their energies to hoarding, speculation, and other kinds of manipulation to protect the value of their assets. Convertibility is essential to link the domestic economy with the world economy; it facilitates the efficient cross-border flow of goods, services, and people. No meaningful import competition or trade along the lines of comparative advantage is likely to take place without the currency being convertible.

4. *Savings, Taxation, Financial Intermediation.* An adequate-to-high level of savings and efficient financial intermediation of the incomes saved by households (the most important source) and businesses into productive investments are essential common features of sustained good economic performance. Efficient investment in physical and human capital is the engine of technical progress and productivity improvements. In the long run, all countries must rely on domestic savings to finance an adequate level of domestic investment. Net borrowing from abroad can assist a country only temporarily and only on the margin.

Countries that have reached a certain level of development need a reasonably sophisticated and competitive banking system. This means a system that is largely private, with investors risking their own money and seeking profits. Savers and investors must have at their disposal an array of attractive financial instruments (e.g., savings accounts, stocks, bonds and the like).

The rate of taxation, direct plus indirect, on business profits and personal incomes must not be prohibitive, that is, it must not be so high as to act as a disincentive to putting forth a strong economic effort by investors, entrepreneurs, managers, professionals, and workers. There is no precise figure on what threshold level of taxation begins to seriously inhibit economic effort; that depends in part on a country's economic circumstances and its culture. But a tax burden that is greater than 50 percent is certain to be constraining; some believe that the threshold rate is considerably lower.

5. *Infrastructure and the Environment.* A sound infrastructure (e.g., a well-functioning system of telecommunications, an adequate network of transportation, good schools, hospitals, and housing) is needed both for the sake of business efficiency and as a vital contribution to a decent standard of living. In addition, people increasingly want the government to help protect the environment. Businesses and people are generally willing to pay for these benefits through some combination of user charges and taxes.

6. *Opportunities for Individual Fulfillment.* Human beings want opportunities to seek personal fulfillment. This means, first and foremost, the political and economic freedom to pursue goals as investors, entrepreneurs, farmers, professionals, and wage- and salary-earners. A pluralistic and relatively stable political system provides the most supportive political environment; economically, the previous paragraphs summarized much of what is needed. In addition, people want a proper and well-managed workplace; an equitable system of personal compensation and a reasonably fair distribution of income and wealth; some degree of employment security; and a back-up system of minimum income maintenance in case of dismissal, old age, or ill health. And since more and more of the simple jobs are being automated (except in the poorest countries), both future employability and personal fulfillment require broad and affordable opportunities for a good education, including continuous upgrading of skills and retraining.

The factors just enumerated are strongly interdependent. For example, competition is not likely to be strong and investment efficient if the means of production are not predominantly private. The voluntary savings needed for investment are unlikely to be forthcoming if the currency is not sound and the taxes are excessive. Foreign competition and integration into the world economy are essential; to achieve them, a convertible currency is needed. These are just a few examples; the list of linkages is extensive.

Legacies of Socialism, Transformation Operations, and Recommendations

To judge what it would take to transform the economic systems and policies of the countries of Central and Eastern Europe into systems that would sustain good economic performance, let us look at the economic legacies inherited by the new governments, using the preceding framework. We also highlight the options and problems of transformation, and make recommendations.[4]

Much of what these countries have inherited in the economic realm, and also their options for transformation, is similar, but certain differences will be noted. The German Democratic Republic, of course, stands out as the country whose absorption into a unified Germany simplifies, first, the intellectual problems of transformation (in terms of not having to spend time searching for an appropriate kind of economic model) and, second, financing its huge costs, which will ease some or much of the pain.

1. *Ownership.* There are not proven ways to develop efficient and fully competitive markets and to motivate producers toward efficiency, customer satisfaction, and innovative behavior in economies where most of the means of production are state-owned. In Central and Eastern Europe, state- or worker-owned enterprises and large cooperatives that function similarly account for much of production (agriculture in Poland and Yugoslavia is an exception) and own an even larger share of productive assets. Privatization is, therefore, a cornerstone of the

transformation. As yet, none of these countries has put in place the full complement of laws and policies that set out firmly the scope, the speed, and the strategies of privatization.

Privatization faces a number of major constraints.

(i) In Yugoslavia, Hungary, and Poland earlier reforms have transferred some of the (not always clearly defined) ownership rights to workers or their elected representatives, in the mistaken belief that this would improve efficiency. Workers often oppose privatization or object to terms of the sale that would be acceptable to a private owner. The two main policy options are to continue to allow workers a say in privatization or to "renationalize" such enterprises, returning to the government all rights of ownership. The latter appears to be the preferred solution on economic grounds, but it is politically exceedingly difficult because it appears to be a step backwards.

(ii) Most businesses will require considerable restructuring before or after privatization because they are typically overstaffed, lack modern production and marketing expertise, and cannot raise sufficient capital in their present state. The arguments for restructuring *before* privatization are that it would be politically more acceptable for the government than for private (especially foreign private) owners to do it, and that revenues from the sale would be greater. The argument for restructuring *after* privatization is that the state may not have the political will or know-how to do the job. My view is that the approach must be country-, sector-, and enterprise-specific.

(iii) There is insufficient accumulated domestic private wealth to find buyers for more than a small fraction of the enterprises to be privatized. Those who have capital often have acquired it in ways the population does not consider legitimate. The main options are (a) to gear the scope and speed of privatization to the availability of private domestic and foreign capital; (b) to give every citizen a share in every enterprise, via holding companies; (c) to finance a portion of the equity acquired by nationals of the country with a special line of credit; and (d) to make large sales and/or placements to pension funds, mutual funds, local governments, insurance companies, nonprofit foundations, and like organizations. Each solution has advantages and problems; some combination of (c) and (d) would seem to be the best strategy.

(iv) Many sectors of production and distribution are dominated by monopolies or oligopolies. Therefore, it is necessary to consider the effects of each privatization on competition.

(v) How should state property offered for sale be valued? One problem is that costs, prices, and the accounting system are arbitrary; a more fundamental one is that private investors are typically willing to pay only a price warranted by the firm's *existing* level of efficiency and earnings, while the population, the press, and most local politicians would like the investor to pay for *future* earnings expected after the improvements. This is as much a political as an economic debate. Many are against privatization, whether because of ideology or envy, and they use economic arguments to support their criticism. A further problem is that in some of the countries, "sweetheart" deals have been consummated between management and buyers through "spontaneous" privatization deals. The recommendation of most experts is that the only way to assure a fair price is to establish, publicize, and enforce fair, competitive, and transparent privatization procedures, and then let the market determine value.

(vi) Should foreign investors receive the same, preferential, or dispreferential treatment as domestic investors? Most experts agree that "national" treatment makes the best economic sense, although simultaneous preferential and dispreferential treatments in certain areas may be justified, some perhaps on a temporary basis.

(vii) Who should get the proceeds and how should they be used? The most basic issue is how much of the purchase price should go to the state and how much should be invested in the enterprise itself? If all proceeds went to the state, would investors be able to pay also for the cost of restructuring? Would that not reduce too much the incentive to bid? But if all or most proceeds went to the enterprise purchased, the investor would then "buy itself" and the state would get little. It seems that no generalized solution can be recommended. The government's revenues from privatization (outright sale, down payments, and debt service) should be used mainly to reduce the government's domestic and foreign debt; a modest share should be contributed to a revolving fund to provide credits for the start-up and expansion of private business ventures.

In sum, privatization faces immense economic and political dilemmas. There are many additional and extremely difficult issues we did not even touch upon, such as handling of the liabilities of an enterprise when only some of its assets are sold, the issues of compensation to owners expropriated after the war, and the privatization of land and housing. All privatization issues are extremely sensitive politically. Most political positions can be justified with economic arguments, some more sound than others. It is worth noting that while the privatization experiences of market economies can offer helpful insights, in Central and Eastern Europe the process has to take place on a much larger scale and in an environment in which much of the capital and many of the essential supporting institutions are inadequate or nonexistent.

2. *Competition and Trade.* In the Council for Mutual Economic Assistance (CMEA) countries, central planning has replaced the market as the main mechanism of resource allocation. The markets that remained or have emerged, mostly in certain consumer goods and services, are functioning inefficiently, especially in the countries where central planning is still pervasive. The chief problem is market segmentation. In some countries most goods and services, in other countries many, are distributed at state-controlled prices and are in short supply. Consequently, all kinds of nonprice mechanisms of allocation have emerged. Therefore, the markets that do operate typically embody large "spillover" effects. This means that the "free" prices on those markets are often much higher than would normally be justified because the money that cannot be spent on the many goods and services that buyers would really have liked to purchase "spills over" into demand for those goods and services that happen to be available. Even in Hungary and Yugoslavia, where past reforms have made planning and the market theoretically coexist and jointly determine resource allocation, the new governments have inherited situations in which the

bureaucratic direction of the economy has remained dominant, even if the instruments used are not those of direct central planning.

The quick freeing of the prices of most goods and services is hampered by the high degree of monopolization of the domestic markets, because norms of fair competition are not well defined, by the almost complete absence of import competition (except in Hungary since 1989 and Poland since 1990), and the prevailing mechanism of intra-CMEA trade.

Creating and maintaining competition requires that the following steps be taken, more or less simultaneously.

(i) Adopt a program of deconcentration (coupled, whenever possible, with privatization) that breaks up those monopolies where technical and economic considerations allow it and where import competition is weak or absent.

(ii) Promote the establishment and growth of small and medium-sized enterprises.

(iii) Establish sound competition policies and institutions, based on freedom to acquire property, for the business firms to enjoy unrestricted entry into and exit from the market, and for labor to freely migrate within the country. Adopt transparent norms of unfair competition, with effective mechanisms for enforcement.

(iv) Create an economic, financial, and legal framework that promotes the development of market forces. Especially important is the creation of efficient capital markets.

(v) Announce a program and timetable for reducing most subsidies. In the enterprise sector, this should be coupled with imposing greater financial discipline on firms and exposing them to domestic and international competition.

(vi) Reform the system of wage determination. One legacy that is highly problematic is that up to one-half of an average wage-earner's total compensation has been paid in the form of free or subsidized goods and services. If subsidies are to be reduced and real incomes are not to decline precipitously, wages and salaries must be adjusted upward. This complicates the problem of wage determination (which is already troublesome because of the absence of real owners to resist unjustified demands for wage increases; their place is taken by bureaucratic regulation). When can wages be allowed to be fully market-determined and whether and how to create a level playing field of wage-setting between state-owned and private firms are two of the many difficult strategic issues of transition.

(vii) Change the existing mechanisms of intra-CMEA trade and finance because a system in which governments direct enterprises in what to export and import is not compatible with a market system, nor is the settlement of transactions in transferrable rubles (TR). In June 1990, the Soviet Union abrogated its network of bilateral agreements to settle its transactions in TR and proposed switching to dollars. This change will almost certainly be introduced next year. Much more difficult is delegating trading decisions to enterprises. Given the Soviet Union's prevailing system and growing economic crisis, it is not inclined to alter the existing arrangements. While in principle it is possible for an East European government to tell its domestic enterprises that they must sink or swim on their own in trading with the Soviets, the impact of such a change on the volume and composition of trade would be very uncertain. To be sure, the economic crisis in the Soviet Union and elsewhere in the CMEA, and the pressures to reorient a significant part of intra-CMEA trade to the world market are, in any event, causing huge shocks and uncertainties for these economies, irrespective of what happens to their system of trading. It is paradoxical that while changing the system of trade would add new uncertainties and burdens in the short run, such a change is in fact unavoidable if a country wants to respond effectively to the crisis in intra-CMEA trade.

(viii) Import liberalization of convertible-currency trade must be the centerpiece of programs creating a competitive economy, allowing prices to be market-determined, promoting exports, and improving the gains from trade. The existing system of mostly implicit quotas and other administrative restrictions must be transformed into tariffs and exchange rate-based "controls" on imports. Import liberalization will be easier in countries like Hungary and Yugoslavia that, over the years, have introduced significant reforms in foreign trade by weakening and eventually disbanding the state's monopoly of foreign trade and by granting foreign trading rights to a growing number of business entities.

3. *Sound Currency.* One of the legacies of a socialist system is pervasive shortages, which means repressed inflation. Shortage is caused by two distinct phenomena. One is the unavailability of goods and services in the right quantities or assortment, or at the time or place needed, i.e., poor matching of demand and supply at micro levels because markets function so poorly. This kind of shortage is largely the result of the economic system. In certain countries, especially in Yugoslavia and Hungary, the reforms introduced in the 1960s were able to reduce shortage but not eliminate it.

The more traditional source of repressed inflation is the result of excess money and credit creation *cum* price controls. The pace of money and credit creation is a policy decision that is not linked closely to the economic system. In recent years, policymakers in Poland, Yugoslavia and the USSR have sinned the most and consequently, by 1990, have come to face the most difficult dilemmas of what to do. If inflation—whether repressed or open—is high, that causes severe damage to the economy for reasons that are too well known to be listed. But wringing out inflation is exceedingly difficult, economically as well as politically, since it involves some combination of large though temporary price increases and restrictive monetary and fiscal policies which cause bankruptcies and unemployment.

Poland has implemented a drastic policy of stabilization. The Balcerowicz program, introduced January 1, 1990, opted for: the rapid elimination of the budget deficit through large cuts in subsidies and other kinds of spending; a very tight monetary policy, initially involving large interest rate increases to restrain credit demand and to create incentives for saving; the closure of unprofitable enterprises, thereby abandoning job security; restricting wage increases to a fraction of the rate of inflation; the virtual elimination of all price controls (except energy and housing); and introducing resident zloty convertibility.

At the time of writing (July 1990), it is too soon to give a definitive assessment of the Balcerowicz program. The economy that the new government had inherited was in such a deep crisis that something drastic had to be done, so shock therapy was perhaps unavoidable. But is obvious (by hindsight as well as foresight) that in Soviet-type economies, inflation is even more difficult to control than in market economies, and for several reasons.

(i) Commercial banks in a Soviet-type economy do not respond to tight monetary policy the way banks do in a market economy. One legacy of the system is that banks do not, as a rule, push enterprises into bankruptcy if their loans are "nonperforming." When the commercial banks were established (in most countries during the last few years, by separating out a part of the former monobank that performed both central and commercial banking functions), they were given an arbitrary portfolio of assets (outstanding loans to enterprises) and liabilities (enterprise deposits) without sufficient reserves to write off the bad loans. And the authorities cannot afford to push into bankruptcy the handful of banks that do operate in these countries.

(ii) The alternative, that of the banks foreclosing on enterprises, is also not practiced. Given the arbitrary nature of costs and prices and the state-imposed supply responsibilities on producers, firms that are loss-making or illiquid are not necessarily those that are truly the worst performers. Even in countries such as Hungary and Yugoslavia where the problem of arbitrary pricing has been improved substantially by reforms, many enterprises are in a monopoly or oligopoly situation. They claim, perhaps with some justification, that their production is essential for supplying the domestic or convertible-currency markets. Given the precarious status of these countries' balances of payments, the threat that their production will be replaced with imports unless they shape up is not credible.

(iii) The way enterprises get around tight monetary policy is "credit queuing." When firms cannot obtain direct financing, they sell to each other on credit. The second enterprise may be unable to pay as well because it is *de facto* bankrupt or because it has itself given pseudo credits to other enterprises, and so on down the line (or "queue"). In a market economy, where enterprises have real owners, there are economic incentives for a creditor to force a nonpaying debtor into bankruptcy, or for the debtor to voluntarily declare himself bankrupt. In a socialist economy, nobody has an economic interest in bankruptcy, or cares if unsound business practices further dissipate the value of an enterprise's assets.

(iv) The only way around these problems (before real owners are found and market institutions are created, which will take time) is for the authorities to institute draconian measures and to let the chips fall where they may. This is what Balcerowicz has done in Poland. But enterprises—not being accustomed to such pressures and not having much experience in how to be flexible, cut costs, and find and adapt to the requirements of new markets—tend to be paralyzed. In the lingo of economists, their supply response is weak. In the meantime, production declines precipitously and unemployment jumps.

The problems just enumerated are not just those of Poland and the countries that must deal with a large stock of excess money and credit. These are problems for all countries during their early stages of transition to a market economy. They too are finding (or will find) it difficult to control the strong inflationary pressures that are generated by:

—reductions of subsidies and the freeing of prices in an economy where producers face insufficient competition;

—increases in nominal wages (including the substitution of subsidies by money wages);

—depreciation of the real exchange rate;

—having to finance the terms of trade losses with the USSR as the CMEA moves to convertible-currency settlement;

—servicing large foreign debts, which reduces domestic supply; and

—increased inflationary expectations.

Thus, it is easy to say that sound money is needed for an economy to perform well, but realize it is very difficult as pressures for substantial price inflation increase and are notably difficult to control.

Although the policy dilemmas are somewhat different in countries where inflationary pressures are very large versus those where they are most moderate, the essential policy question is still whether to try to get inflation out of the way quickly by a more or less once-and-for-all increase in the price level (bunching together as many as possible of the factors that account for inflation), which involves a willingness to suffer the political price and run the risk that inflation may get out of control altogether, or restrict prices to increase more gradually, which makes the process more protracted and the medicine perhaps less effective.

In either case, it is essential that no time be lost by the authorities in creating or strengthening those monetary, banking, and financial institutions and instruments that are essential for monetary policy to be effective.

Sound money also means a convertible currency. There are many different kinds of convertibility: for residents and nonresidents, for the enterprise and the household sectors, and for current- versus capital-account transactions. Most important, I believe, are (a) that domestic enterprises be able to buy the foreign currency to pay for imports; (b) that foreign investors be able to convert their local earnings and repatriate the capital invested; and (c) that foreign tourists could readily obtain the local currency at a single exchange rate and that the inflow be channeled (via the authorities or via a foreign exchange market) into imports and debt service rather than into the mattresses or foreign bank accounts of currency speculators.

Should the exchange rate be fully market-determined by letting it float; should the authorities fix the rate and try to maintain it; or should they opt for an intermediate solution, such as frequent but small adjustments?

The main advantages of the floating rate are that the authorities need not maintain large reserves and that there will be a single exchange rate in the economy. Its disadvantage is that under conditions that typically prevail in these countries during the early stages of transformation, the market will assign an extremely low value to their currencies relative to their purchasing power. This makes not only exports but domestic assets also very cheap to foreigners. That, in turn, creates or exacerbates the political problem of foreign investment and also feeds inflation.

The advantage of a fixed exchange rate (depending on where the rate is set) is that it mitigates the above problems. Its disadvantage is that fixed rates are not possible to maintain without economic policies that support them, and without adequate reserves.

Poland, as part of its program of economic stabilization and liberalization, decided on a very substantial devaluation, eliminating the huge difference between the official and grey market rates, and then trying to keep the rate fixed. Hungary also has a fixed exchange rate regime, periodically adjusted for inflation differentials, but its official rate values the forint significantly higher than the rate prevailing on the parallel (grey) market, so it has a *de facto* multiple exchange rate system.

4. *Savings, Taxation, Financial Intermediation.* One legacy is the very large share of the German Democratic Party that is channeled through public coffers—60 to 65 percent—which of course has to be covered by taxes. Extensive redistribution in the form of transfers and subsidies to and from enterprises and households is the main reason why the share is so high.

The net voluntary savings of households (the sector that throughout the world provides the bulk of savings) is much lower in socialist economies than in market economies for the following reasons.

—The share of personal income in the total income of the population is low because too much is distributed centrally.

—The share of personal income saved is also lower than in comparable market economies because, until now, governments have provided full pensions, free education and health care, and job security. International studies of what motivates household savings show that the precautionary motive (the individual's desire to weave a personal safety net) is the most important. Therefore, one reason that governments in Central and Eastern Europe need to substantially reduce their cradle-to-grave systems of support is to encourage voluntary savings; another, of course, is that many of those programs are dysfunctional and too costly to be affordable without imposing prohibitively high individual and business taxes.

—In some of the countries the level of household debt is very high because automatic entitlements to subsidized loans for housing have created the incentive to assume the largest possible mortgages. In Hungary, for example, housing subsidies alone (mostly on the interest rate) consume 15 percent of the central budget.

—Real (or perceived) interest rates on household savings have been negative until recently, in all the countries; it is still the case in some of the countries.

—The absence of opportunities to buy stocks, mutual funds, and other financial and real assets has reduced the incentive to save for investment purposes.

In such systems, much of the economy's large savings is generated by way of very high direct and indirect taxes. For example, Hungary today has a 53 percent payroll tax (43 percent paid by the employer and 10 percent by the employee), a 50 percent marginal income tax rate, a 40 percent corporate profits tax, a value-added tax of up to 25 percent, plus many additional specific excise taxes. The government then decides, politically and bureaucratically, how to allocate its large revenues. This helps explain why these economies have such notoriously low efficiency of investment.

The main objective of fiscal policy during the transition should be to reduce significantly the tax burden on producers and households while, at the same time, balancing the budget. To encourage capital formation, retained earnings should be taxed at significantly lower rates than distributed earnings, and savings and capital gains should be granted preferential tax rates. Other exemptions should be reduced and the tax systems restructured to conform to international standards.

There is an urgent need in all these countries to strengthen the financial system by allowing much greater scope for competing private financial intermediaries, including foreign-owned ones. Private financial intermediaries are essential for improving the efficiency of investment allocation. There is a role for governmental institutions and programs, but they too should be run in a businesslike fashion.

5. *Infrastructure and the Environment.* Two areas where the all-powerful governments of the socialist countries should have outperformed their counterparts in market economies are building and maintaining infrastructure and protecting the environment. How paradoxical that especially in these areas all the centrally planned

economies governments have performed so disgracefully poorly. The extent of environmental degradation is immeasurably worse in Eastern than in Western Europe. This is explained partly by the priority placed on development of mining, metallurgy, the chemical sector, and other heavy industries, and partly by simple inattention. Infrastructure has also been neglected. One reason for the worsening crises in these economies is that by now they have "used up" much of the infrastructure inherited from before the war.

It is urgent that environmental regulations be tightened and enforced and that a long-term program of clean-up be adopted and financed, partly from external sources. Practical considerations suggest that infrastructure should be opened up to foreign investment since the budgets of these countries are simply not in a position to devote the resources needed to develop and maintain infrastructure at the desired level of efficiency.

6. *Individual Fulfillment.* It was already mentioned that one of the legacies is a cradle-to-grave system of social programs. This seemingly attractive public aim has turned out to stifle personal responsibility and to generate a large bureaucracy and many regulations, with a great deal of corruption and waste. The transformation must begin with a recognition that governments cannot fulfill people's lives through pervasive interference, however well-intentioned. Governments' responsibility is to create a stable economic and political environment and the confidence-inspiring institutions that permit individuals to fulfill their own lives.

Although it is up to each country to adopt the kind of social support systems it wants and can pay for, the direction of the needed changes includes the following.

—Subsidies for consumer goods and services should be reduced or eliminated.

—Housing, which in most countries represents a huge and unsustainable drain on the state budget and causes serious distortions in fiscal and monetary policies, needs to be privatized and much of it commercially operated. Unsustainable terms of outstanding mortgages must be changed.

—Only a minimum level of pension should be compulsory and operated by a government agency; private pension systems should supplement it.

—Retirement ages should be adjusted to reflect demographic realities, the country's labor force needs, and ability to pay the state's pension obligations.

—To improve the efficiency of health care delivery, the cost of routine medical services and related prescription drugs should be reimbursed only in part, except for patients with very low incomes. Privately operated health care should be allowed to compete with socialized health care as an incentive to provide high-quality service at affordable prices (more or less the Canadian system).

—The above-recommended changes in programs, together with the elimination of job security for all, will require the establishment of a new kind of social safety net which should rest on two pillars: unemployment compensation and assistance to the needy.

—The systems of education as well as training must be changed, for the sake of better individual fulfillment and also to prepare the kind of labor force their economies need today and even more in the future. In all these countries, access to higher education is much too exclusive and restricted. The proportion of young people in secondary and especially in tertiary education is much lower than in the Organization for Economic Cooperation and Development countries and it must be raised. Today's curriculum (in education as well as in training) tends to prepare for skills that are defined too narrowly and are often obsolete. The curriculum must be broadened, putting more emphasis on basic skills, interdisciplinary studies, communications, and greater individual choice of courses and flexibility of thinking.

Conclusions and Implications for Western Policy

Transition involves changes in the economic system, strategic economic decisions, and economic policy choices.

The most important strategic decision is the sequencing and speed of transition. In countries that face an unusually large macroeconomic disequilibrium, the highest priority must be given to stabilization. This may require what in popular parlance is known as shock treatment. Immediate attention must be paid also to introduce those reforms in the institutional framework that are needed to make stabilization policies effective.

One of the great unknowns is whether it is possible to significantly improve economic efficiency as long as most enterprises remain state-owned and partly worker-managed. The only option is to try, since there is no easy and quick solution to privatization. The key must be to design and then hold firmly to a program, with a timetable, that introduces greater competition and eliminates the hope for case-by-case state support for the enterprises that are failing.

Concerning the pace of systemic transformation, the place for caution is at the policy deliberation phase, weighing the alternatives, the likelihood of achieving intended and unintended consequences, sequencing choices, and modes of implementation. Measures should be packaged into large bundles because the economy operates as an organic whole and not as an unrelated collection of bits and pieces. Packaged into large bundles, the linkages in the system can be relied upon to effectively enhance every other action.

Moving rapidly also makes political sense: to prevent a consensus that forms immediately after the elections from dissipating before a large package of measures is implemented and results become evident—probably a minimum of two to three years. Any large program, such as privatization and foreign economic liberalization, will take years to implement, even at maximum speed.

Agreements with the international and regional organizations, such as the International Monetary Fund (IMF), the Group of 24, and the European Community, can help a government sell a tough program domestically by holding out the promise of such economic benefits linked to program implementation as, for example, some type of association with the European Community. International agreements can also enhance the government's credibility that its program will be implemented.

Credibility also means not raising unrealistic expectations. If government policies lack credibility, are hesitant, are full of unworkable compromises, then managers and individuals will refuse to change their behavior to fit the new policies. This, itself, can undermine transformation. For certain countries, such actions also undermine international creditworthiness.

Tremendous obstacles stand in the way of governments following the suggestions outlined in this essay. In some countries, the first problem is that of insufficient credible and mobilizable expertise to design good programs. Even in countries where the requisite expertise can be found (e.g., in Hungary), there is this question: will the experts—many of whom have cooperated with the previous and rather liberal Communist governments and/or are associated with one of the opposition parties that is not a member of the governing coalition—be listened to by the authorities or be pushed aside as "politically unreliable"? There are signs that this is happening, which is a great pity. None of these countries has a second set of first-rate experts waiting in the wings, as there are in the industrial countries.

The most fundamental constraints are political. Throughout the region, the population has high expectations that changing the political system will bring about quick economic improvements. Democratic elections, with new and old parties competing for power, tend to reinforce these expectations with promises that are unrealistic. In some cases the promises are made because politicians do not understand the situation, in others out of sheer demagoguery. To make matters even more difficult, there are many politically influential persons who still believe in their heart of hearts that some kind of a third road is a viable option and behind the scenes are pushing the policymakers to take it. Not infrequently, such persons hide behind market economy slogans.

Newly elected politicians in all these Central and Eastern European countries face an extremely difficult and unpleasant situation. They have inherited the sorry legacies of the previous regime. These legacies require the new governments to take a series of tough actions. Most have unpleasant consequences for the economic well-being of the population, and thus for political stability in the short run. The fruits of those actions will ripen only years later, perhaps after the next, or after the next-to-the-next, election. It is realistic to expect that wise statesmen are (or will soon be) governing these countries? This essay began with a statement that the body politic in four of the countries has made a *seemingly* firm commitment to become a market economy. Yes, they genuinely want to become like the social market economies of Western Europe. But this does not mean that they are also willing to take the tough steps that will lead there.

I have only a single thought concerning Western policy toward these countries. We should give them substantial economic help, but tie our assistance to tough and internationally well-coordinated conditionality. Some energy should be devoted to public education that explains the requirements and pitfalls of transformation and the rationale of conditionality. Although the United States does not have much money to offer, it should rely on its intellectual and political leadership to direct a Western consensus on these issues.

Governments in Central and Eastern Europe should be expected and nudged to make the tough economic changes that experts agree are needed. Otherwise they will not and should not last long, and western assistance will have been wasted.

NOTES

1. The distinction among the three models derives from my discussions with and the writings of the distinguished Canadian economist, Sylvia Ostry. See, for example, her *Governments and Corporations in a Shrinking World: Trade and Innovation Policies in the United States, Europe, and Japan* (New York: Council on Foreign Relations, 1990) and her co-authored article in the May 1982 issue of the *OECD Observer.*

2. The idea of market socialism was first put forward in the 1930s by theoreticians in the West, such as Lange and Taylor, largely in response to the Great Depression. Next, it was revived in a

rather special form in Yugoslavia (socialist self-management) in the early 1950s as an alternative to the Stalinist model. Then it was resurrected in the 1960s by reform economists in Poland, Czechoslovakia, and Hungary. Perhaps the fullest expression of market socialism was the blueprint of Hungary's New Economic Mechanism, much of it introduced in 1968. Until the late 1980s, reform economists in all the Communist countries were politically constrained from advocating any system change more radical than market socialism. Today, as the political constraints have lifted in many of the former Communist countries and as negative experiences with models of market socialism accumulate, a growing number of specialists, including the author of this essay, have doubts that market socialism is a viable economic system. In some cases, market socialism refers to the temporary economic system that will be in place during the period of transition to a genuine market economy, when state-owned enterprises will still be dominant and the government will have to play a central and pervasive role in managing the transition.

3. For further details, see Masaru Yoshitomi, "Micro- and Macro-Foundations of Japan's Economic Success," in Andras Koves and Paul Marer (eds.), *Foreign Economic Liberalization of Hungary and the CMEA and International Experiences* (Boulder, CO: Westview Press, forthcoming). I have also benefited from discussions with Seiichi Masuyama of the Nomura Research Institute (London) about Japan's economic system.

4. From here on, this essay relies extensively on the findings and recommendations presented in *Hungary in Transformation to Freedom and Prosperity: Economic Program Proposals of the Joint Hungarian-International Blue Ribbon Commission* (Indianapolis and Budapest: Hudson Institute, 1990).

Soviet Economic Reform Under Gorbachev

Trials and Errors

Abram Bergson
Harvard University

Paper presented
October 17, 1990

Since he became Party General Secretary on March 11, 1985, Mikhail Gorbachev has been presiding over a veritable revolution in the Soviet Union. It is but one facet of the upheaval occurring that, while continuing as Party General Secretary, he derives his authority over Soviet affairs in no less degree from his status as President, a post newly created on March 14, 1990 and to which he was elected by an extra-party legislative body.

Gorbachev has been endeavouring to achieve a restructuring—or *perestroika* as the process is now known everywhere—of Soviet society generally, but he has been especially concerned to reform the economy. As one need only refer to the daily news to become aware, the improved performance he is seeking has turned out to be decidedly elusive. A summary review, however, may provide perspective on a complex and ever-shifting scene. It may also provide needed background for judging the possible import of further dramatic reform measures currently being debated, though regrettably I cannot probe these in any depth here.[1]

I

We must have in mind some more or less familiar facts concerning the state of the Soviet economy when Gorbachev became General Secretary. At that time, the Soviet economy was still organized much as it had been under Stalin, with the means of protection predominantly publicly owned. The collective farm, prevailing in a considerable segment of agriculture, was an outstanding exception to this rule, ownership there being cooperative rather than public. But the distinction was largely nominal, and enterprises of both sorts were administered through the famous system of central planning that in essentials had originated with Stalin.

Soviet central planning has become notorious for its cumbersome bureaucratic character, but tempos of growth under Stalin and for a time under his successors were quite respectable by Western standards. Nevertheless, such tempos did not persist. Soviet national income, which was still growing by as much as 5.1 percent yearly in the 1960s, has slowed markedly since that time. By 1981-85, the tempo had fallen to 1.9 percent (Table 1). Western students of the Soviet economy generally consider unclassified CIA estimates as more reliable than similar measures of growth released by the Soviet government. Soviet official data also show a marked decline in growth, but growth rates are almost always higher than recorded by the CIA.

While growth rates were once high, output expansion was expensive. Under an extensive growth process that Stalin initiated, the government relied primarily on the sheer multiplication of inputs of labor and capital to increase output.[2] This process contrasts to the intensive one familiar in the West, where output expansion tends to be generated in good part by technological progress and gains in efficiency more generally. Although that requires outlays for research and development, the costs of additional output under the intensive process tend to be distinctly less than under the extensive one.

The difference is material, for the more costly the expansion the more limited the rewards for consumers. And under Stalin such rewards were limited indeed, but the Dictator died on March 5, 1953.

Table 1
Selected Economic Indicators, USSR, Average Annual Rate of Growth
(percent)

	1961-70	1971-75	1976-80	1981-85	1986-90 (plan)
1. Net material product (NMP), Soviet official[a]	6.4	5.1	3.9	3.1	4.1
2. Gross national product (GNP), CIA estimates[b]	5.1	3.7	2.1	1.9	c
3. Gross fixed capital investment, Soviet official[d]	6.9	6.8	3.5	3.5	4.9
4. Industrial output, Soviet official	8.5	7.4	4.4	3.7	4.6
5. Industrial output, CIA estimates[b]	6.6	5.9	2.4	2.0	c
6. Agricultural output, Soviet official[e]	c	2.5	1.8	1.0	2.7
7. Agricultural output, CIA estimates[b,e]	c	1.4	0.4	(-) 0.6	c
8. Real income per capita, Soviet official	6.5	4.3	3.4	2.1	2.7
9. Consumption per capita, CIA estimates[b]	3.8	2.9	2.0	1.9	c

SOURCES: Soviet official data and plan goals, TSSU (1986) and earlier volumes in the same series; *Pravda*, March 9, 1986; June 19, 1986; June 20, 1986; John Pitzer (1982), CIA (1985, pp. 64ff; 1989, pp. 45, 58ff); Gertrude E. Schroeder and M. Elizabeth Denton (1982). For consumption, 1981-85, and agricultural output, 1976-85, unclassified CIA data supplied to author.

a. Utilized for consumption and accumulation.
b. Output valued in 1970 prices for growth rates for 1961-75 and in 1982 prices for growth rates for 1976-85.
c. Not available.
d. CIA estimates essentially accord with Soviet official data.
e. Yearly growth rate of average for five-year period over average for previous five-year period.

If only out of a concern for morale and as incentives for an increasingly educated and sophisticated labor force, Stalin's successors have felt impelled to moderate his onerous priorities.

While consumers have benefited as a result (Table 1), that moderation has meant a slowing of expansion in the volume of investment, and that has contributed in turn to the slowdown in output growth. As a cause of the slowdown, however, the retardation of investment volume growth has only compounded the impact of another, widely reported trend. The Soviet labor force, which grew by 1.4 to 1.8 percent yearly during the 1960s and 1970s has more recently been increasing at less than half that pace.[3] Although output growth has slowed, it has remained of the costly, extensive sort. Indeed, it may, if anything, have become even more costly than it was before.[4]

The Soviet growth process nevertheless enabled a once backward country to become, in time, a military superpower. But in 1985, when Gorbachev became General Secretary, Soviet *per capita* consumption was little more and very possibly less than 30 percent of the U.S. *per capita* consumption.[5]

In the USSR, the immediate pre-Gorbachev years have come to be referred to as years of stagnation (*zastoi*). Regarding the economy, that must be considered as hyperbole to a degree, but Gorbachev had good reason to be concerned upon being elevated to General Secretary. As we may judge from his actions as well as pronouncements, he was, in fact, deeply concerned.

II

The economic reform measures Gorbachev has initiated have been numerous and diverse, but a principal aim has been to restructure industrial planning. It seems clear that that is also a sphere in which his efforts thus far have not been especially fruitful.

This is particularly evident in respect of the attempt to upgrade the role of the industrial enterprise *vis-a-vis* that of central planning authorities and in the process to substitute market-type for bureaucratic control over enterprise operations. Under Soviet central planning, bureaucratic control over the enterprise has never been as complete and control of a market type never as lacking as often supposed; but, after a period of experimentation, the government in June and July 1987 adopted legislation supposedly providing for increased reliance on market-type control at the expense of bureaucratic control.[6]

The legislation affirms that "the enterprise independently works out and confirms its plans." The plans in question, it is explained, are to be those for five years as well as one year. This was, on the face of it, quite a shift from previous practice.

The grant of authority to the enterprise is qualified, however, and as it has turned out, the qualification has been rather important. Among other things, the enterprise is obliged to accept so-called "state orders" (*goszakazy*) for its output that are submitted to it by the superior ministry. Such orders apparently were intended to serve the ministry as a transitional means of directing and coordinating enterprise activities. Initially controlling a substantial share of the enterprise's output, the state order was supposedly to give way rapidly to wholesale trade.

In fact, the state order immediately became and still is a major instrument by which ministries control the activities of subordinate enterprises. As Prime Minister Nikolai Ryzhkov acknowledged in May of this year (*Pravda*, May 25, 1990), "for the most important products, government orders the basic part of output—up to 95 percent."

Why was so little accomplished in this sphere? One explanation often given in the USSR as well as the West stresses vested interests of superior bureaucratic agencies. Concerned about their hierarchical and material status, ministerial personnel in particular, it is said, seek whenever possible to maintain control over the enterprise.

There is doubtless some truth in that view, but under the 1987 reforms the ministry is still responsible for the performance of enterprises subordinate to it. At least, it is accountable for fulfillment of its own plan. In this circumstance, even personally disinterested ministry officials must hesitate to relax fully their grip on the enterprise.

Then, too, in order for wholesale trade to effectively supersede bureaucratic control, it must function as a market. That is to say, enterprises must be structured to respond appropriately to prices of their inputs and outputs, and prices in turn must fluctuate appropriately in response to the resulting enterprise supply and demand.

A principal aim of the 1987 reform measures was to subject the enterprise to increased financial discipline, which previously had often been wanting, and in doing so to make rewards more dependent than before on financial results, especially profits. Insofar as such rearrangements materialized, the enterprise should have been oriented broadly to respond to prices as in a market environment.

But financial discipline seemingly continues to be an elusive desideratum for the Soviet enterprise. Indeed, there may well have been some retrogression in this sphere, with the enterprise, perhaps as a counterpoint to its subjection to state orders, being even less observant than before of financial constraints. Particular difficulty apparently has been encountered in the control of wages. Unplanned growth of the wage bill accounted, for example, for more than half of an extraordinary increase of 9 percent last year.[7] As we shall see, the unbridled growth of wages has been costly in more ways than one.

But for an effective market, not only must enterprises be subject to appropriate financial constraints, prices must be appropriately determined. For industrial wholesale prices, that was far from the case before 1987, and it still is. Rather than being determined by market forces, industrial wholesale prices are, for the most part, fixed by the government. Under the 1987 reforms, the principles observed in this sphere were to be altered in various ways, but prices were not to be revised accordingly until January 1, 1990. The price revision has since been further deferred, so that prices are still much as they were in June and July 1987, when the reforms were initiated.

That is also to say that they can have had little to do with the scarcity values that an effective market generates. Rather, they have, at best, reflected costs of earlier years—usually costs of 1982, when the last major price revision was carried out.

The failure of the government to revise industrial wholesale prices, if not to free them from control has been one of the most serious deficiencies of its efforts thus far to reform central planning, in my opinion. The more or less arbitrary prices have made a mockery of the government's efforts to rationalize and invigorate financial controls over the enterprise. Such controls have, in any case, proved no more effective than they were before.

While seeking to enhance the authority of the industrial enterprise, the government has also been in the process of restructuring the enterprise's internal administration. It has since retreated, however, from one particularly interesting 1987 innovation. The arrangement for workers' election of the manager, Yugoslav-style, that was adopted in 1987 has since been abandoned.[8] As Prime Minister Ryzhkov has explained, the manager of a state enterprise is appropriately appointed by the state whose interests, as owner, he represents.

III

While for Gorbachev the reform of industrial planning has been a cardinal concern, economic restructuring has called for action much beyond that. Indeed, reform in another related sphere, not so much stressed initially, may well have come to be considered of comparable urgency to that of industrial planning. The shifts in property relations being instituted could prove more rewarding, though here too the road to reform has not been exactly smooth. While the shifts occurring have attracted much notice in the West, they are not always well understood.

Early on (November 19, 1986), the Gorbachev administration declared to be permissible a wide variety of private enterprise activities that previously had been prohibited or were at least legally dubious. Subject to local licensing, private enterprise was legally sanctioned in such diverse fields as handicraft manufacture, construction and repair, and various other services. Diverse activities were still excluded, however, and individuals who are normally employable in the public sector were supposed to work on their own account only after hours. Employment of hired labor was expressly forbidden.[9]

Even as thus restricted, this legislation represented a distinct break with the past, but it was enacted in a milieu long conditioned to hostility to private enterprise. The restrictions maintained on private enterprise activity must be seen in that light, and so too must be the government's decision to levy onerously progressive taxes on any elevated private enterprise incomes.[10]

Not too surprisingly, enactment of the new legislation on private enterprise has not been followed by any wholesale shift to such activity. Nearly four years later there were still only 500,000 persons registered for employment in private enterprise (*Pravda*, July 7, 1990).

A near counterpart of such private enterprise, however, has fared decidedly better. While nominally a producers' cooperative (co-op) the collective farm, as I noted, is practically a state enterprise. That is also true of the consumers' co-op that continued through the years to function in trade, primarily in rural localities.

After much public discussion, however, the Gorbachev administration has declared the cooperative to be a basic form, along with state enterprise, of socialist economic organization, and has acted to codify its widespread use as a substantially autonomous entity in industry, trade, and services. Here too some activities have been expressly excluded, and members must participate actively in the cooperative's work; employment of hired labor is allowed, however.[11]

While ideologically on a somewhat different plane from individual private enterprise, the cooperative has by no means enjoyed an easy acceptance. But in the critical sphere of taxation, its members, after much controversy and vacillation, have come to be treated on a par with workers in state enterprise.[12] The upshot has been a rapid increase in employment in co-ops, the number of persons engaged having reached by now five million (*Izvestiia*, July 29, 1990) or some 3 percent of the labor force.

The activities of co-ops are diverse. Particularly noteworthy is the fact that they are beginning to take advantage of further novel legislation allowing them, along with other interested parties, to acquire control over productive assets by leasehold contract. In the process, they have even taken over, under contract, shops or departments of state enterprises. Under the lease agreement, they usually produce for sale to the lessor enterprise.[13] While such arrangements are so far of very modest dimensions quantitatively, they have been seen in the USSR as a possible basis for extensive privatization of state enterprise (FBIS, Dec. 20, 1989, p. 47).

Leasing has been envisaged in that way regarding not only industry, but agriculture. Indeed, some Soviet economists have seen the lease arrangement as a way to supplant collective and state farm agriculture with not only genuine co-ops but individual family farms. Here too, though, such restructuring has, to date, materialized only on a minute scale (*Report on the USSR*, July 14, 1989; Brooks, 1990a; 1990b; *Pravda*, July 29, 1990).

Promotion of private enterprise is also the apparent objective of a still more novel measure just enacted. As well as being very new, the law on joint stock companies is very complex. But, through an appropriate distribution of shares, it evidently could be, like the lease, an instrument for privatization of state enterprise, and its use in that way has been urged by no less a person than Nikolai Petrakov, an advisor to Gorbachev. Having enacted legislation of this sort, the government, not surprisingly, seems to have finally abandoned its prohibition of employment of hired labor by private enterprise.[14]

I alluded to the prevalence in the USSR of a hostility to private enterprise. Once deeply rooted ideologically, such hostility is now in the process of erosion. At least it no longer shapes public policy as it once did. By no means, however, has it been rendered nugatory. Its influence can still be seen in residual legislative disabilities and restrictions to which I have referred, and even more in the administration of relevant statutes. Often left to republican and local governments, such administration has tended to compound obstacles to newer enterprise forms.[15]

Private enterprise, moreover, continues to be affected by a related factor that is at the same time unfavorable as well as favorable. Soviet planning is in the process of being reformed, but it is as yet not radically different from what it was previously. That is to say, it is still a system where prices are notably distorted and shortages notably frequent.[16]

In this environment private enterprise, predictably, has often had to cope with daunting difficulties, especially in materials procurement, and has often experienced very favorable opportunities, such as provided by high prices for products in short supply. In these circumstances, private enterprise, also predictably, has often engaged in bribery and other illicit activities, and frequently earns large rewards which, even when derived from legitimate activities, are easily seen as inordinate. The Soviet leadership is apparently committed to the extension of private enterprise, but that can be expected to continue to be, as it has been, a troubled process.

IV

We have considered the number of major economic reforms initiated since Gorbachev became Party General Secretary in March 1985. In seeking to grasp the import of *perestroika* for the economy, we must now turn to a further development—though it is properly viewed as a retrogression rather than as a reform.

Under central planning, while the government relied generally on bureaucratic procedures to coordinate and direct economic activities, it also made limited use of market-like arrangements for that purpose. Among other things, it traditionally distributed consumer goods to households through a retail market. There households were able to purchase consumer goods with money they received in wages in return for services rendered or in other ways. For the most part, goods were made available to households at fixed prices in state retail shops, but households could also obtain foodstuffs in free markets where collective farms and their members disposed of surplus supplies.

Households could acquire consumer goods in these ways, insofar as such products were available. In fact, they were by no means always available, for with state shops the preponderant outlet and supplies and prices for the most part determined through a bureaucratic process, the retail market did not work very well. Lately, it has hardly worked at all.

Never entirely absent from the Soviet scene, queues and empty shop shelves have now become pervasive. Some scarce products are rationed locally or distributed preferentially to their workers by employing establishments. For the rest, the ruble has been aptly held to be not real money, but a kind of lottery ticket, generally redeemable for goods only with luck and perseverance.

The breakdown of the Soviet consumer goods market has been widely reported. As rarely understood, however, there has been no sharp fall-off in consumer goods supplies. Provision of some food-stuffs is down, and supplies of other products—cigarettes are the latest example—have fallen off irregularly. Per capita consumption overall, however, according to the CIA (CIA, DIA 1990) is little, if at all, below pre-Gorbachev levels.

Supplies, nevertheless, are in fact markedly short of demand. That is due chiefly to a mushrooming government budget deficit, which last year reached 92 billion rubles or 10 percent of the Gross National Product. The government has been funding the deficit in good part by inordinate currency emissions.[17] Lax wage and credit controls, to which I have already referred, have compounded the inflationary development.

The government, however, has chosen to hold down most consumer goods prices, so that the inflation has been primarily repressed rather than overt. Thus, the major imbalance of demand and supply that has materialized has resulted not so much in price increases as in involuntary household savings in the form of cash and savings deposits. The savings have been involuntary in the sense that goods have not been available on which to spend them.

The breakdown of the consumer goods market has, needless to say, been onerous for consumers, but it has also been costly otherwise. By eroding labor incentives, as widely reported, it has begun to cause what in the USSR is euphemistically called a "falling off of interest in work."

I referred earlier to the difficulties posed for reform by the continued prevalence of economically irrational wholesale prices. It has not helped that at the artificially low levels at which the government has held them, retail prices too have been notably divorced from scarcity values. For food products the prevailing low retail levels could be maintained only through provision of subsidies which in the aggregate were nearly as large as the entire government budget deficit (FBIS, Sept. 28, 1989).

Why has the Gorbachev administration allowed such a doleful conjuncture to materialize? Soviet commentary is not as incisive on that very relevant question as one might wish, but long accustomed to a consumer goods market that was not exactly flawless, the leadership, one surmises, was not as alert and sensitive initially as it might have been to the deleterious effects of the budgetary indiscipline in which they indulged. If only tardily, they have now come to grasp clearly enough the unfavorable results of such a financial policy, and have been seeking in diverse ways to repair the damage.[18] But, as we know from our own experience, balancing a budget, once it is greatly out of balance, is a neat trick, not easily accomplished.

V

Gorbachev had reason enough to try to reform the Soviet economy. How has the economy performed since then? In view of the breakdown of the consumer goods market, the question in a sense answers itself, but it is still of interest to observe that, as estimated by the CIA, growth of output overall actually accelerated in 1986 (Table 2). That was due chiefly, however, to a bumper farm crop. Since 1986, growth has tended to be even slower than in 1981-85. The agricultural harvest this year has reportedly been exceptional again, but industrial output is now declining absolutely, and the fall could be marked.[19] The ambitious targets of the 13th five-year plan (1986-90), set early on by the Gorbachev administration (Table 1), are evidently far beyond reach.

If Gorbachev has not yet succeeded in reinvigorating the Soviet economy as he set out to do, that is not very surprising. The political revolution that he has also been actively promoting has rightly been acclaimed in the West and clearly enjoys wide support in the USSR itself, but the resultant disintegration of totalitarianism has often brought with it notable indiscipline and disorder, which are hardly favorable to economic performance. The recent, much-noted Soviet Republic assertions of sovereignty are only one, albeit important, manifestation of this new Soviet politics.

Table 2
Growth of National Income, USSR
Annual Average, 1981-85 and 1986-89, and Annually, 1986-89
(percent)

	Net Material Product (NMP), Soviet official[a]	Gross National Product (GNP), CIA
1981-85	3.1	1.9
1986-89	2.2[b]	2.2
1986	1.6	4.1
1987	0.7	1.3
1988	4.6	2.2
1989	c	1.4

SOURCES: Table 1; TSSU (1989, p. 16); CIA-DIA (1990).
a. "Utilized for consumption and accumulation."
b. 1986-88.
c. Not available.

In pondering the experience to date under Gorbachev, one must consider too that his five years in office is after all a very brief interval in which to transform an economic system that was some seven decades in the making. A surge in growth would have been nice, but as Soviet economists themselves have properly cautioned, was hardly to be expected.[20]

Granting the extenuating circumstances, however, questions may be raised about the nature and implementation of the reform program that the government has initiated. One must wonder particularly whether the egregious inconsistencies in the measures to restructure industrial planning could not have been foreseen and avoided. Among Western students of the Soviet economy, a questions is also often raised about the underlying strategy, especially the priority accorded the relatively intractable task of reforming industrial planning over that of privatization of agriculture and services.

I have been referring to Soviet economic performance under Gorbachev as it is manifest in overall growth. Unsatisfactory as the record has been from that standpoint, it has been much less satisfactory in respect of the rudimentary task of distributing among households available supplies of consumer goods. Costly for the consumers, the retail market breakdown is probably also beginning to have an adverse impact on production and growth. And here too it is permissible to ask whether, with more skillful management at the highest level, a more favorable outcome might not have been achievable.[21]

But, disappointing though economic reform has been, it need not be irrevocably so. Do not some of the reform measures, especially those in the sphere of ownership, have potentialities yet to be effectively exploited? If, on the other hand, there has often been less than proficient management, is that not remediable? What, in any event, are the prospects that economic reform will become a more rewarding endeavor in due course?

The answers must depend in good part on the outcome of discussions now in progress, to which I alluded at the outset. The dismal results of reform thus far have, not surprisingly, provoked wide-ranging debate over its future course. The outcome of such discussion is still not too clear, but one perhaps need not wait for t's to be crossed and i's to be dotted on resultant measures to anticipate that restructuring favorable to private enterprise and the market already in progress will continue, very possibly at an accelerated pace. The imbalance in the consumer goods market could be ameliorated in the process, but that seems especially conjectural.[22]

Unfortunately, all signs also point to a continuation of the indiscipline and disorder lately experienced. Such behavior could easily become more prevalent under the impact of ongoing political shifts, especially the still unlegitimated transfer of power under way from the center to the republics. It is difficult to avoid the conclusion that the economic reinvigoration that Gorbachev has been seeking will likely continue to be elusive for some time to come. The USSR, it has been said, is now at the edge of the abyss. That is doubtless hyperbole, but the short-term outlook for the Soviet economy is hardly bright.

NOTES

1. With the kind permission of Dr. Armand Clesse, I sometimes draw on a paper, "Economics of Perestroika" which I presented at a conference in Luxembourg in 1988, and which was subsequently published in Armand Clesse and Thomas C. Schelling, eds., *The Western Community and the Gorbachev Challenge.* Baden-Baden, Nomos, 1989. I allude in the text to an ongoing debate on the future course of economic reform, and in conclusion allow myself to speculate on the outcome of this controversy. These very general remarks still seemed sufficiently apt not to require revision when news came (on the day of the lecture!) of Gorbachev's recommendations to the Supreme Soviet on the matter at issue.

2. See the measures of "factor productivity" in Bergson (1989a; ch. 6); CIA (1988, p. 63).

3. The decline in labor force growth is due to reduced increases in labor participation rates as well as demographic factors. See Fesbach (1983); Rapawy and Baldwin (1982, Part 2), and CIA (1987, p. 70).

4. See Bergson (1989) and CIA (1988).

5. Essentially an extrapolation from Schroeder and Denton (1982) and Bergson (1989a, ch. 4), using data in CIA (1987, pp. 53, 66); *Economic Report of the President* (1988, p. 279).

6. For the relevant decrees and related legislation, see *O korennoi...* (1987). For an illuminating discussion of this legislation and its antecedents, see Hewett, Winston et al. (1987); Schroeder (1987); Hewett (1988); *Joint Economic Committee* (1987); Desai (1989). Note that the key measure on the state enterprise, enacted on June 30, 1987, was not to become effective until Jan. 1, 1988.

7. *Pravda*, Jan. 28, 1990. The government instituted in the fourth quarter of 1990 an onerous tax on inordinate increases in wages in industries other than those producing consumer goods (*Pravda*, Aug. 11, 1990), but the intended discouragement of such boosts hardly materialized. That has been, it seems essentially because of the elliptic interpretation of the scope of exempt industries.

8. See FBIS, Dec. 14, 1989, pp. 42-43; *Izvestiia*, June 12, 1990. The 1987 legislation also gave to the workers' collective the option to have their incomes determined, in the Yugoslav manner, as a residual share after nonlabor expenses and taxes. This arrangement too, I believe, is no longer allowed.

9. For the Nov. 19, 1986 decree, see *Pravda*, Nov. 21, 1986. On the decree and its application in practice, see also Blough, Muratore, and Berk (1987, vol. 2); Roucek (1988); Pomorski (1988).

10. In its latest formulation (*Pravda*, May 6, 1990), the tax on, say, a full-time handicraftsman is not as progressive as it was formerly, but the marginal rate still rises quickly from 20 percent on incremental income at the 3,001 ruble annual income level to 60 percent on such income in excess of 6,000 rubles. For wage earners and salaried workers, too, the marginal tax rate rises to 60 percent, but not until the annual income reaches 36,000 rubles. Even so, the tax on such workers has become more progressive than it was formerly.

11. For the key statutes, see *Pravda,* June 8, 1988; FBIS, October 23, 1989, Nov. 16, 1989, July 12, 1990. On excluded activities, see also FBIS, Jan. 5, 1989; *Report on the USSR,* Feb. 3, 1989.

12. See *Pravda,* May 6, 1990. All-union legislation on the taxation of cooperatives as such, as distinct from their members, also seems not to discriminate against such organizations, but republican authorities are apparently allowed a degree of discretion to do so, if they should so wish (*Izvestiia,* June 29, 1990).

13. Leasing of productive assets is not new in the USSR, but the government seems to have modified regulations for its wide use only recently, initially in a law of April 7, 1989, and then apparently in a revised version in a law of Nov. 23, 1989 (*Pravda,* April 9, 1989, December 1, 1989).

14. The basic law (*Ekonomika i zhizn'*, No. 27, July 1990) should be read together with additional measures on ownership (*Pravda,* March 10, 1990) and on small business (FBIS, Aug. 10, 1990, p. 43). See also *Report on the USSR,* May 11, 1990. Petrakov apparently envisages a distribution of shares primarily among state institutions, such as banks and local governments, but they would also be made available to private individuals (*Moscow News,* No. 26, 1990).

15. On the restrictive republican and local policies and practices, and on the disabilities of private enterprise more generally, see Plokker (1990). Also illuminating regarding the status of the co-ops in particular is FBIS, July 13, 1989, pp. 71-74.

16. In the consumer goods market, of particular importance to private enterprise, the price distortions and shortages have, if anything, become more pronounced under Gorbachev. See below, Section IV.

17. Ofer (1990) and the related comment of Bergson.

18. Most notably in the program presented by Ryzhkov to the Supreme Soviet in May but not approved by that body. An outstanding feature was the proposal to sharply increase prices of consumer goods, including grossly subsidized food products. See FBIS (May 25, 1990).

19. The state statistical office reports (*Pravda,* July 29, 1990) that Net Material Product declined by 2.0 percent during the first six months of 1990 compared with the corresponding period in 1989. Reference is to "national income produced" rather than "national income utilized," but the statistical office has now begun to report also on the GNP, apparently as that is understood in the West. For the first half of 1990, that shows a decline of 1 percent. These figures for the first half, which are probably inflated, would not register the exceptional harvest, but by the same token should indicate a decline in nonfarm output. There are many indications that that decline is accelerating.

20. Soviet economists seemed to be optimistic initially, though, in supposing that the transformation could be completed in a relatively brief period (FBIS, Feb. 12, 1988, pp. 66ff, May 11, 1988, pp. 81ff, May 23, 1988, pp. 81ff).

21. It may not be amiss to note that for the writer this is not just hindsight. I stressed the fiscal incongruities at a symposium in Moscow in December 1987. What I said, though, was apparently no surprise to at least one Soviet participant, Leonid Abalkin.

22. On the principal alternative programs being considered, see FBIS (May 25, 1990); Ryzhkov (*Pravda,* Sept. 12, 1990); Shatalin et al. (*Izvestiia,* Sept. 4, 1990).

References

Aganbegyan, Abel. *The Economic Challenge of Perestroika.* Bloomington, IN: Indiana University Press, 1988.

Bergson, Abram. *Planning and Performance in Socialist Economies: The USSR and Eastern Europe.* Boston: Unwin Hyman, 1989a.

———. "Economics of Perestroika." In *The Western Community and the Gorbachev Challenge,* eds. Armand Clesse and Thomas C. Schelling. Baden-Baden: Nomos Verlagsgeseltschaft, 1989b.

Bergson, Abram, and Herbert S. Levine. *The Soviet Economy: Toward the Year 2000.* London: Allen and Unwin, 1983.

Blough, Roger, Jennifer Muratore, and Steve Berk. "Gorbachev's Policy on the Private Sector." Joint Economic Committee, United States Congress, 1987, pp. 261-271.

Brooks, Karen. "Agriculture and Five Years of Perestroika." Staff Paper Series, Department of Agriculture and Applied Economics, University of Minnesota, February 1990a.

———. "Lease Contracting in Soviet Agriculture in 1989," *Comparative Economic Studies* 32, 2 (Summer) 1990b, pp. 85-108.

CIA (Central Intelligence Agency). *Handbook of Economic Statistics 1985.* Washington, DC, 1985.

———. *Handbook of Economic Statistics, 1987.* Washington, DC, 1987.

———. *Handbook of Economic Statistics, 1988.* Washington, DC, 1988.

———. *Handbook of Economic Statistics, 1989.* Washington, DC, 1989.

CIA, DIA (Central Intelligence Agency, Defense Intelligence Agency), *The Soviet Economy Stumbles Badly in 1989,* a paper presented to Joint Economic Committee, United States Congress, April 20, 1990.

Desai, Padma. *Perestroika in Perspective.* Princeton, NJ: Princeton University Press, 1989.

Economic Report of the President. Washington, DC: Government Printing Office, 1988.

Ekonomika i zhizn'. No. 27, July 1990.

Feshbach, Murray. "Population and Labor Force." In *The Soviet Economy: Toward the Year 2000,* eds. Abram Bergson and Herbert S. Levine. London: Allen and Unwin, 1983, pp. 79-111.

FBIS (Foreign Broadcast Information Service). *Daily Report Soviet Union.*

Hewett, Ed A. "Gorbachev's Economic Strategy," *Soviet Economy,* 1, 4 (October-December) 1985, pp. 285-305.

———. *Reforming the Soviet Economy.* Washington, DC: Brookings, 1988.

Hewett, Ed A., Victor H. Winston, et al., "The First Soviet Economy Round-table," *Soviet Economy*, 3, 4 (October-December) 1987, pp. 273-359.

Izvestiia.

Joint Economic Committee, United States Congress. *Soviet Economy in the 1980s.* Parts 1 and 2. Washington, DC: Government Printing Office, 1982a.

———. *USSR: Measures of Economic Growth and Development, 1950-1980.* Washington, DC: Government Printing Office, 1982b.

———. *Gorbachev's Economic Plans*, vols. 1 and 2. Washington, DC: Government Printing Office, 1987.

Moscow News.

Ofer, Gur. "Macroeconomic Issues of Soviet Reforms." In *NBER Macroeconomics Annual 1990*, eds. Olivier Blanchard and Stanley Fischer. Cambridge, MA: MIT Press, 1990.

O korennoi perestroike upravleniia ekonomikoi. Moscow: Politizdat, 1987.

Pitzer, John. "Gross National Product of the USSR, 1950-80." In *USSR: Measures of Economic Growth and Development.* Washington, DC: Government Printing Office, 1982.

Plokker, Karen. "The Development of Individual and Cooperative Labour Activity in the Soviet Union," *Soviet Studies*, 42, 3 (July) 1990, pp. 403-428.

Pomorski, Stanislaw. "Privatization of the Soviet Economy under Gorbachev." Berkeley-Duke Occasional Paper No. 13, October 1988.

Pravda.

Radio Liberty Research.

Rapawy, Stephen and Godfrey Baldwin. "Demographic Trends in the Soviet Union." Joint Economic Committee, United States Congress (1982, Part 2), pp. 265-296.

Report on the USSR (Radio Liberty).

Roucek, Libor. "Private Enterprise in Soviet Political Debates," *Soviet Studies*, 40, 1 (January) 1988, pp. 46-63.

Schroeder, Gertrude E. "Anatomy of Gorbachev's Economic Reform," *Soviet Economy*, 3, 3 (July-September) 1987, pp. 219-241.

Schroeder, Gertrude E. and Elizabeth M. Denton. "An Index of Consumption in the USSR." Joint Economic Committee, United States Congress (1982).

TSSU (Tsentral'noe statisticheskoe upravlenie). *Narodnoe khoziaistvo SSR v. 1985g.* Moscow: Finansy i statistika, 1986, and other volumes in the same series.

———. *Narodnoe khoziaistvo SSSR za 70 let.* Moscow: Finansy i statistika, 1987.

Reconstructing the
Soviet Planned Economy

Joseph S. Berliner
Russian Research Center

Paper presented
February 20, 1991

Six years ago the Soviet Politburo chose Mikhail Sergeyevich Gorbachev to lead the Communist party and the country. He must have
been regarded by his colleagues as a firm and decisive political leader
committed to the system he was selected to lead. He must also have
been congenial to the wing of the party leadership that felt a profound
dissatisfaction with the performance of the economy and was open to
new ideas, even radical ideas, for changes that might improve its performance. There is nothing in the record, however, to suggest that Gorbachev himself had any particular conception of what those changes
ought to be.

The one idea he had been associated with for a long time was the so-
called "brigade method" of production organization. The idea was to
organize the workforce in each farm and factory in such a way that
each group of workers, called a brigade, would be responsible for a
clearly defined production task from beginning to end. For example,
instead of paying some workers for plowing a field, others for planting
it and others for harvesting it, one brigade would have the responsibility for all three tasks. The brigade would then be paid on the basis of
the final quantity harvested. The workers would therefore have a material interest in seeing to it that the plowing and all the other operations
were done well; this is in contrast to the traditional method in which
tractor drivers were paid for plowing a piece of land and could not be
held accountable if poor plowing were responsible for a poor harvest.
Gorbachev was a great promoter of the brigade method, both as party

leader of his province of Stavropol, and later as a Politburo official in charge of agriculture.

The language of economic management at the time distinguished two methods of organizing economic activity. One was the "administrative method," in which people were told what job to perform and how to perform it by a manager or planning official. The other was the "economic method," which was designed to provide direct material incentives in a way that would motivate workers to do what the planners wanted them to do without having to be monitored at each stage. To be a radical in those days was to be a supporter of economic methods, stressing individual incentives over planning directives. The brigade method is an example of an economic method, and Gorbachev, as a promoter of economic methods, must have represented the enlightened radical wing of the party leadership.

This background is useful as a benchmark from which to judge the distance that the Soviet economic debate has progressed in those six years. Only in a few abstruse economic journals did the term "market" appear from time to time, and the term "privatization" was not to be found at all. Neither of those concepts could have been in the minds of the Politburo when the vote on the new General Secretary was taken. The man they elected must have distinguished himself not by a vision of a radically different Soviet economic system, but by his bold expression of dissatisfaction with the performance of the economy and by his advocacy of economic rather than administrative methods, which was the mark of a farseeing party leader of that time.

The reasons for the leadership's dissatisfaction with the performance of the economy are well known and need little elaboration. The primary reason was the relative decline of the USSR in the economic-growth competition since the Second World War. In the late 1950s, the Soviet growth rate was more than twice that of the United States, and it exceeded all the Organization for Economic Cooperation and Development countries except West Germany and Japan. Those were the years in which the Soviet leadership confidently believed that it was only a matter of time before their country would surpass the United States and outdistance the entire capitalist world. In the subsequent decades, the growth rate declined in many countries, but the decline was more rapid in the USSR. Consequently, by the end of the 1970s the Soviet growth rate was exceeded by the United States and by more than half of the OECD countries.[1] Moreover, the capitalist countries of the Pacific Rim were growing at such phenomenal rates that their *per capita* incomes were likely soon to overtake those of the USSR. The Soviet leadership no longer contemplated the gratifying prospect of surpassing the capitalist world, but instead now faced the dismal possibility of losing the economic capability of maintaining all the foreign and domestic commitments undertaken in support of their superpower status in the past.

The leadership also shared a certain view about why the growth performance of the economy had deteriorated so badly. Soviet economists had developed a mode of analysis of the sources of growth similar to the analysis of factor productivity that was developed in the West in the 1960s.[2] The Soviet analysis distinguished between "extensive" and "intensive" growth. The principal source of extensive growth is a growing stock of capital (as well as labor and land), while the principal source of intensive growth is the improved quality of the capital stock deriving from technological progress. The comparative analysis of economic growth in these terms showed that while the growth of the capitalist countries was primarily of the intensive kind, deriving from technological progress, Soviet growth was primarily of the extensive kind, deriving from heavy investment in increasing the capital stock. The meaning of this result was that the USSR had missed the boat of modern technological progress, and that was the major cause of declining growth performance relative to other countries. This line of analysis was eventually accepted by the top leadership of the country, and the acceleration of technological progress had become a major theme in high-level government reports.

These were the economic concerns of the Communist party leadership in 1985. They elected a General Secretary who looked as if he could shake the economy up in ways that would restore the high growth rates of the past and would accelerate technological progress to a rate appropriate for a great power.

Soviet Economic Performance

The poor performance of the Soviet economy has been widely reported and is well known in the West. This, however, is only one side of the story. If this side of the story says that things were pretty bad, there is another side of the story that says things weren't all that bad. This second side has not been widely reported in the press, perhaps for the same reason that lawful behavior is not widely reported but criminal behavior is. In both cases the preoccupation with pathology can give a distorted impression of the state of the society. In the Soviet case, the persistent reporting of the bad news, unrelieved by any good news, led to such hyperbolic expressions as "crisis" and "basket case." In the early 1980s, for example, there were reports that the new Reagan administration believed the Soviet economy to be so close to collapse that the need to respond to the Strategic Defense Initiative would be enough to push it over the edge.

That view lacked a sense of perspective. Things can be tough without being ready to fall apart. In fact the Soviet economy in 1985 was still reasonably productive and stable, despite its poor record relative to the leading economies of the world. One need only look at the USSR today to recall how stable and productive it was six years ago. Two pieces of evidence may be cited.

Professor Abram Bergson calculated Soviet labor productivity to be 58 percent of that of the United States in 1975. This compares with the United Kingdom at 75 percent, Spain at 68 percent, and Japan at 64 percent of the United States. Some portion of the Soviet lag is due to the fact that the capital per worker is smaller in the USSR than in the other countries. Drawing on the experience of a group of capitalist countries, Bergson estimated Soviet labor productivity at about 73 percent of that to be expected in a capitalist country that had the same capital per worker as the USSR.[3] The finding is consistent with the common view that the Soviet economy's performance is significantly inferior to that of the capitalist economies, but on the other hand it does not depict an economy that is headed for disaster.[4]

With respect to technological attainment, the most authoritative study is that of a research group of engineers and economists at the University of Birmingham, in England. Their study covered a range of industrial products such as chemical engineering, steelmaking, and computers. They found that in most fields of technology the USSR lagged behind the West, with the largest lags in the most rapidly advancing technologies like microelectronics. However, there was no evidence that the gap widened during the period 1956-1976.[5] During those years technology was advancing very rapidly in the West, and since the Soviets managed to keep the gap from widening, their rate of technological progress must have been substantial. That is not a satisfactory performance from the perspective of the Soviet leadership, for at those relative rates of technological advance the USSR would remain forever behind. There is also some evidence that the gap did widen somewhat after 1976, particularly in the crucial field of microelectronics. Yet the picture is one of a country with substantial technological capability, though not in the major league of world technological advance.

The significance of this second side of the story is that the Soviet leadership did not launch this massive economic transformation out of dire necessity. It was not an economy in shambles, and they were not under siege by hungry masses demanding change. It was not like China after Mao, where actual starvation occurred in parts of the country and the desperate peasants themselves dissolved the communes and divided the land into family farms. It was not like Poland in 1989 with inflation running at 1000 percent a year and the shops bare of many foodstuffs. Unlike those countries, the decision to undertake a radical change in the economic system was motivated by the conviction of the leadership that the continuation of business as usual would cause the USSR to fall continuously behind the rest of the world. By the end of the century, it was increasingly said, the Soviet Union would have become a Third World country.

Gorbachev's policy is therefore properly viewed as a "revolution from above," in the tradition of Peter the Great three hundred years earlier. That perspective—that it is a revolution from above—explains a great deal about the way in which the transition has evolved.

First, it explains the extensive resistance, both active and passive, to the program of economic restructuring. The old system still delivered on some of its original promises, such as the elimination of capitalist-type unemployment. Virtually no factory had been closed down in the USSR since its inception, and no Soviet worker knew what it was like to "lose a job." Earnings were low, but bread and meat prices and apartment rents were also extremely low, so that everybody could afford them. Quality and availability were poor, but no one starved or went homeless. It was not a hungry population clamoring for a new system that, for all its promises, would bring unemployment and an end to the low prices on bread and housing. Gorbachev did succeed in marshaling the support of like-minded political and military leaders, and he kindled the enthusiasm of liberal intellectuals; but there was no large constituency demanding change, and there were large social groups, such as workers and bureaucrats, who felt threatened by radical change.

Second, it explains why the new government, committed to radical economic change, had only the vaguest idea of what kinds of changes it wanted to bring about. Past governments had encouraged research on ways of improving the operation of the economic system, but never having doubted the fundamental soundness of that system, they had not authorized research on alternative systems. If there was a desert in the USSR, it was not in the economy or in the technology, but in the stock of economic ideas. The most radical ideas that had appeared in print were recommendations for making greater use of such economic methods as price and profit incentives, instead of administrative methods. No doubt many economists secretly harbored more radical ideas than that, but they were not part of the open economic discourse.

Third, and perhaps most important, it explains the other major component of the transformation—democratization; particularly it explains *glasnost*, or freedom of expression. Gorbachev has sometimes been criticized for having weakened central political controls before economic decentralization had been accomplished. The example of post-

Mao China, as well as South Korea and Taiwan, is thought to demonstrate that the combination of tight central political control with extensive individual economic freedom is the best formula for rapid economic transformation.

Gorbachev believed, however, that that formula would not work in the USSR. For generations the party had preached the superiority of the Soviet socialist planned economy, the wisdom of the party's leadership, the correctness and necessity of Stalin's heritage, and the freedom of Soviet citizens from the evils of unemployment and exploitation that plagued the capitalist world. With that history, it was impossible to announce one day that the system was now to be totally dismantled and replaced by one suspiciously similar to capitalism in many ways. The people had to be convinced that they had been lied to all these years—that Stalin had been a tyrant, that the system he introduced had destroyed rather than released the creative energies of the masses, that the Soviet people had fallen in lethargy and moral decay, and that the capitalists do a lot of things right and it was necessary to learn how to do them, even if the learning will be painful.

This is why *glasnost* was thought to be necessary. If Gorbachev had sought to undertake a radical change without loosening the political and ideological reins, he would have had to rely on the existing instruments of power, the party and the economic bureaucracy. These organizations had proven to be largely reform-resistant in the past, even to the modest within-system reforms introduced by past General Secretaries. In no way could they be counted on to execute the directives of a new General Secretary whose slogan was not simply the improvement of the traditional economic system, but the complete reconstruction—*perestroika*—of that system into a new system that would have little use for planners and ministries.

I think Gorbachev was right. In the USSR at least, there could be no economic transformation without weakening the power of the party and the ministerial bureaucracy, without liberalization of personal expression, and without coming to terms with the past.

Glasnost has been politically costly. It has released powerful forces of nationalism, separatism, xenophobia, and reaction. Nevertheless, without that political liberalization it would not have been possible to have gotten to the point today where a popularly elected Soviet Parliament is debating not *whether* to introduce private property and markets, but the *speed and extent* of privatization and marketization.

The proposals now before Parliament are so radical that the restructuring efforts of the past six years look like ancient history. They were of crucial importance, however, in bringing the economy, and the debate about the economy, to the point it has reached today. I would like to discuss two developments that are fundamental in the restructuring of the economy: first, changes in the rules of property ownership; and second, changes in what the Soviets call "the economic mechanism" referring to planning or markets. I will then conclude with a brief discussion of two other developments that have greatly complicated the transition to a restructured economy and may possibly bring the process to a halt. They are the onset of inflation, and the political conflict between the national and the republic governments.

Legalization of Private Property

The first significant break with the past under Gorbachev was the legalization of certain limited forms of private ownership of productive property. The most widespread form is the cooperative, in which two or more persons form an enterprise that operates much like our partnership. Individual persons and their families are also permitted to engage in economic activity, but the cooperative has become the dominant form of the new private enterprise.[6]

Cooperatives are permitted to buy and own productive equipment, to hire wage labor, to produce and sell goods and services, and to determine their own prices rather than sell at the low state-controlled prices. The cooperators may retain the profit as their private income after paying taxes. They are typically engaged in such activities as the production of clothing, restaurant services, small-scale construction, taxis, and repair services for automobiles, plumbing, consumer durables, and so forth.

Cooperatives have encountered intense hostility from many sections of the public. Part of the reason is a general antipathy toward the economic activities conducted by persons who are thought of as middlemen, speculators, merchants, exploiters, and capitalists—sentiments long cultivated by Soviet propaganda but having deeper roots in traditional Russian culture. But there are more specific reasons.

The prices charged to the public are substantially higher in the cooperatives than in state stores. One reason is that their costs are higher. Cooperatives have to pay higher prices for their own supplies because they provide higher-quality goods and services. They also pay higher prices for many of the supplies they need than state enterprises have to pay.

In addition to higher costs, cooperative prices are higher because they often sell in markets where state-supplied products are sold at controlled prices far below market-clearing price levels. Cooperative prices, which have to cover costs, must therefore be sold at prices that are well above those in state stores. To the Soviet public, however, the cooperators are simply price gougers, and the growing shortages of goods in the state shops are thought to be due to the cooperatives that buy the goods cheap and sell them dear in their own shops. The income of cooperators are also much higher than the average, and they are not shy about flaunting their new wealth in conspicuously high living.

In addition to a hostile public, the cooperatives also face hostile local government officials who see in them a threat to what was formerly their monopoly of power. These officials have waged an effective rear-guard battle against the cooperatives, by denying them licenses, raising their tax rates, and impeding their access to supplies and to building space in which to conduct their business. Inevitably, relationships of this sort spawn corruption, including payoffs to political and police officials and protection money to ordinary hoodlums, all of which further increases the cost of doing business and therefore the prices that cooperatives charge.

After this litany of obstacles, one might guess that very few cooperatives have succeeded. On the contrary, despite these handicaps, the cooperative movement has grown dramatically. The number of people employed in cooperatives grew from a few thousand initially to about 4.5 million people last April. They are now reported to be producing almost 5 percent of the gross domestic product. There is no doubt that the consumption levels of many Soviet citizens is significantly higher because of the co-ops, although higher-income citizens have benefited more than the less well-off. The movement also gives reason to believe that there are substantial untapped entrepreneurial talents in the Soviet population, contrary to the opinion of some Soviet observers that 70 years of socialism has destroyed that talent.

More significant than the growth in the number of cooperatives is the accumulation of experience. Millions of Soviet citizens have learned how to figure out what other people want to buy, how to acquire materials, equipment and labor, and how to figure costs. They have learned how to borrow from the State Bank, and some cooperatives have banded together to form their own cooperative banks. Some have learned how to attract and work with foreigners in joint ventures; it was a cooperative that almost pulled off the notorious export of military tanks that created something of a sensation last year.[7] The quiet and steady accumulation of business experience by the cooperatives may in the long run prove to be the major development during these six years in preparing the country for the move to a market economy.

Until last year, the legalization of cooperative and individual enterprise was the major change in the property ownership rules of the economy. There was little echo in the USSR of the tempestuous movement in Eastern Europe to proceed with the privatization of the huge sector of state-owned enterprises. That has now changed. The so-called "500-day plan" proposed to change the ownership forms of almost all of the state-owned enterprises. Smaller workshops and retail stores were to be auctioned off, to be run as private enterprises. Larger state enterprises were to be converted to joint stock companies, the shares to be transferred eventually to citizens. State ownership would continue only in defense industry and in natural monopolies such as railways and electric grids.[8]

The 500-day plan was adopted by the Russian republic, but only a considerably watered-down form of it was adopted by the USSR

Supreme Soviet. Privatization is becoming a major issue dividing the liberals from the conservatives. In light of the conservative swing in Soviet politics at present, clearly supported by Gorbachev, privatization does not have a bright future at this time. Barring a radical shift in political power, the legalization of private enterprise rather than privatization of state enterprise is likely to be the extent of the restructuring of ownership rules in the Soviet economy for some time to come.

The 1987 State Enterprise Law

The second fundamental feature of an economic system is the mechanism employed for coordinating the transactions of the millions of enterprises and economic agents. Modern history knows only two mechanisms of this kind—markets and planning. Before the Russian Revolution, markets were the predominant mechanism in modern economies. Economic planning was the great Soviet contribution to the repertory of economic institutions.

For 70 years, Soviet ideology had preached the evils of capitalist markets and the superiority of socialist planning. Again, it took the policy of *glasnost* to launch the debate in which many people learned for the first time how badly the planning mechanism had in fact operated, and how and why markets do many things better than planning. The growing pressure for marketization finally bore some fruit in the crucial State Enterprise Law of 1987.

The law declared that state-owned enterprises should thereafter decide for themselves what to produce, rather than be directed by the planners on what to produce. They should also negotiate with other enterprises for their supplies, rather than have their supplies allocated to them by the planners. They should compete with each other for sales, and in making their production and supply decisions they should seek to maximize their profit. If fully implemented, those provisions of the law would have the effect of substantially replacing the central planning mechanism by a market mechanism.

That was July 1987. Marketization has proceeded to some degree, but Soviet economists are uniformly agreed that it has not proceeded very far. The reasons may be seen in two of the many problems encountered in the implementation of the law.

First, to protect the economy against the possibility that the new and untried market system might fail—not an unreasonable precaution—the planners were given the right to issue to enterprises plan directives of the old kind—now called "state orders"—if in their judgment the new and untried system might not produce the required quantities of all commodities.

In fact, many enterprises felt unready to take the plunge. On the production side, they were used to producing what they were told by a ministry to produce, with the ministry then arranging for the sale of their products. Now they were told to figure out for themselves what and how much to produce. What if they produced too much and could not sell it? They were used to the ministry informing them how much fuel, iron and other supplies they were to receive, and who their suppliers would be. Now they were told that they must find their own suppliers, in an economy where everything was in short supply. What if they could not find suppliers willing and able to sell them as much as they needed?

To protect themselves from such pitfalls, many enterprises pleaded with their ministries to issue them state orders for as much of their production as possible. Producing in response to a state order guaranteed that the ministry would accept responsibility for the sale of the product and also arrange for the required supplies to be made available. The ministries, in turn, were happy to issue state orders liberally because the new law placed them in an administratively impossible situation: they continued to be responsible for the performance of their enterprises, but they were deprived of the power to tell their enterprises what to do.

The result was that in the first year in which the new law was in operation, state orders—which are equivalent to the old central planning—accounted for a huge proportion of industrial output, ranging from 90 percent to 100 percent in some industries.[9] Despite the criticism of reformers, most output continues to be produced under central planning rather than market conditions. Former Prime Minister Ryzhkov expressed the hope that production under state orders could be reduced to 40 percent by 1991,[10] but there seems little likelihood that so sharp a decline in central control will be brought about so rapidly.

The story reflects the anxieties and the conflicting forces associated with the transition from planning to markets. But such anxiety ought to be expected in the circumstances. It is indeed something of an achievement that many enterprises are now operating without state orders for some or all of their output and are evidently learning how to market their products and how to contract for the delivery of their material supplies. Auctions, bazaars, fairs and barter trade are some of the spontaneous developments of new institutions that may prove to be the forerunners of genuine markets.[11] This part of the story of the 1987 law is one of an initial setback, but also of the beginnings of a gradual accommodation to the needs of a market system.

The second problem of the 1987 law derives from the fact that during the transition the economy is neither fully marketized nor fully planned, but is some combination of the two. Under such circumstances, some highly undesirable phenomena can occur.

For example, in response to the law's instruction to enterprises to maximize profit, managers set about seeking the most profitable items to produce, and dropping the production of items that yielded losses or very little profit. As a result, some products began to disappear from the shops, with unfortunate consequences. The saddest case occurred when hospitals suddenly discovered that they were unable to obtain disposable hypodermic needles. It turned out that the director of the only enterprise producing syringes, wishing to be a good citizen under *perestroika*, found that they were not profitable and switched to the production of more profitable items. Similar sudden shortages occurred in the case of soap, matches, aspirin, cigarettes and other items.

The reason for these episodes is that the state still controls most prices, of which there are many millions. It is impossible for the state price controllers to set all prices at the levels that will induce profit-maximizing managers to produce just those things that consumers

most desire. Under central planning, the inability of the price controllers to set such prices was of little importance, because the ministry
would simply order its enterprises to produce soap and syringes,
regardless of their profitability. But when the ministry no longer has
that right, production can go badly awry if prices do not respond
quickly to shortages.

The lesson of the State Enterprise Law is that before markets can be
expected to work well, a great many different institutional arrangements must be in place: legal institutions for enforcing contracts, banking and credit institutions, accounting and auditing institutions, price
determining arrangements, and so forth. If some of them are not yet
functioning, the market system can perform very badly; indeed an
incomplete market system might perform worse than a coherent central
planning system.

Some disruptions of these kinds are an unavoidable cost of transition. It is for this reason that some people advocate a very rapid transition from planning to markets—the faster the better—to minimize
these costs. Too rapid a transition has its own costs, however, for it
leaves too little time to prepare the ground for markets to work properly. Unfortunately, there is very little experience in this type of transition from which informed judgments may be made. In 1917, Russia
was the guinea pig for testing the world's first transition—from markets to planning. Today, the USSR is again a guinea pig, this time for
testing the world's first reverse transition—from planning to markets.

Inflation

Under the best of circumstances, the story of the progress of *perestroika* should end here, with an account of changes in the two fundamental features of an economy—ownership rules and the economic
mechanism. Unfortunately, other changes have occurred in the country
that have greatly complicated the transition. The two that are of greatest significance are the onset of inflation and the conflict between the
union and the republics.

Before 1985, Soviet fiscal and monetary policy had been extremely conservative. The government budget was roughly in balance from year to year, and wage payments were under tight control.

Around 1987, things began to come apart. Government expenditures continued to rise while revenues began to decline. Some of the causes were beyond the government's control, such as the Chernobyl nuclear plant accident and the Armenian earthquake. Others were the consequence of ill-advised government policies, such as the fervent anti-alcoholism campaign that sharply reduced government revenues from the alcohol tax. The State Enterprise Law, which permitted enterprises to retain a larger share of their profits, resulted in a further reduction in government revenues.

The consequence was a rapidly increasing government budget deficit, which amounted to about 10 percent of the gross national product in 1989.[12] Unable to finance the deficit by domestic or foreign borrowing, the government did what beleaguered governments often do in such straits—it printed new money.

As a result the money incomes of the population increased more rapidly than the production of the consumer goods and services. In a market economy, that would have led to price increases—open inflation. Marketization of the Soviet economy, however, has not yet extended to the determination of retail prices by market forces. Prices are still set by the government and remain fixed for long periods of time. The rising money incomes of the population are then expressed in the form of repressed inflation. The weekly delivery of meat to the state store, which formerly may have lasted for six days, is now all sold out after five days, then after four days. The population soon learns to shop early in the week, the queues grow longer, and eventually the week's delivery is sold out the day it arrives. That is the dynamic that has led to the grim phenomenon of empty shelves in the state stores while the unspent cash balances in the hands of the population continue to rise.

These effects of repressed inflation have been disastrous for the progress of *perestroika*. It has led to a declining sense of consumer welfare, which many people blame on the abandonment of tight central planning in favor of markets and cooperatives.[13] It has reduced consumer resistance to the evasion of price controls by profit-seeking state enterprises. It has fostered the expansion of the black market. The declining value of a ruble of wages had eroded labor discipline and work incentives. It has aggravated the hostility to the cooperatives whose market-based prices diverge more and more from the fixed subsidized state-store prices.

The opinion is universal that the restoration of macroeconomic equilibrium is an absolute precondition to any further progress in *perestroika*. The government has, in fact, set forth a program for reducing the deficit, consisting primarily of a reduction in expenditures, but with some increases in revenues. Despite this broad agreement, it is difficult to be sanguine about the prospect for arresting the inflationary pressures for two reasons, both political.

First, no government finds it easy to eliminate a budget deficit, especially when it involves political commitments to expenditures that entail a deficit as high as 10 percent of GNP. Even strong governments find that difficult, and the Soviet Union's government is particularly weak at this time.

Second, all the plans for *perestroika*, even the radical 500-day plan, exclude so-called "essential consumer goods" from the list of commodities whose prices are to be set free to reach market levels. The government is to continue to fix the prices of foodstuffs and housing, presumably at the same low levels that prevailed in the past. Those low prices, which the population has long grown to regard as one of the few benefits of socialism, are maintained by government subsidies. The subsidies on agricultural products alone are now roughly equal to the entire budget deficit.[14] Neither the government nor its principal critics are prepared to bit the bullet of food price increases. Gorbachev himself remarked that such price increases "would make the whole people take to the streets and topple any government."[15] Indeed, the loudest protest against one timid attempt to raise food prices came from Boris Yeltsin, who represents himself as being impatient with the slow pace of *perestroika*.

One can only conclude that the political leadership across the entire spectrum is scared to death of the popular reaction to an increase in basic consumer prices. They do not have the confidence of the Solidarity-based government in Poland that they could persuade the people of the necessity of bearing the hardships that would be involved in such measures as the introduction of a market-pricing system for all commodities and the restoration of a balanced budget. As long as these conditions prevail, the prospect of any significant expansion of market relationships seems quite remote. It is ironic that this monetary problem, which has nothing to do with *perestroika* itself, has mushroomed into a major obstacle to its further progress.

Political Legitimacy

One of the fruits of political liberalization is the intense conflict between the national government and the member republics. The conflict is a compound of a number of elements, including ethnic violence in places like Armenia and Azerbaijan, separatist forces in places like the Baltic republics, and demands for sovereignty in such republics as Russia and the Ukraine.

There can be no more fundamental requirement for a stable society than general agreement on who has the legitimate right to govern. In the absence of such agreement the society is prey to chaos or civil war as contending groups struggle for power, each in the conviction of the rightness of its cause. As the political conflict ripens, it takes its toll on economic activity. An order from the national government that prices on luxuries be raised was not enforced in the Russian republic by order of its government. An increase in the price of meat in Russia caused a flurry of shipments of meat from the Ukraine to Russia. The Ukrainian government responded by forbidding the export of meat to Russia. Ukrainian officials claim that Russia then retaliated by cutting off shipments of oil supplies to the Ukraine.[16] Similar protectionist skirmishes have been breaking out all over the union. Foreign investors have already acknowledged increased uncertainty in business dealings because one cannot be sure that the Soviet signatory of a delivery contract will be sustained as having had the lawful right to sign it.[17]

Neither Soviet history nor world history offers much hope that the deep problem of political legitimacy will be easily solved. One must expect very turbulent times ahead, perhaps for many years. Until that issue is somehow resolved—if only provisionally—the prospect is for little further progress in economic transformation and further deterioration in economic performance.

Conclusion

After six years in office, the Gorbachev government has made a modest start in the transition from the central planning to the new economy of the future. Instead of universal state ownership of enterprise, a lawful place has been made for private enterprise. Instead of total central control over the output of state enterprises, some portion of that output is now produced by the decisions of the enterprises themselves, not bound by "state orders."

To those Soviet citizens who saw the election of the new General Secretary as the beginning of a truly radical transformation of the economic system, the results thus far are disappointing. Moreover, the economy today is in a much poorer condition than before 1985. Total output and consumption *per capita* are in fact higher than in 1985,[18] but because of the disorder in consumer goods markets, there is a general feeling of being worse off than before.

If one is of an optimistic disposition, there are some signs of things happening that may help the transition move forward. Several million people in the new private sector are learning the managerial and financial skills of business enterprise. Thousands of others have engaged in joint ventures with foreign capitalist firms and are absorbing the techniques of international management and finance. Profits are being earned and private money capital is accumulating that may one day serve to purchase the assets of some privatized state enterprises. Managers of some state enterprises are learning how to do business with each other, instead of taking orders from their ministries, and the rudiments of market relationships are spreading. Some republican governments are seeking to curb protectionist impulses, and tentative accommodations are sometimes arrived at even between such contenders as the national government under Gorbachev and the Russian republican government under Boris Yeltsin.[19] Historians may some day conclude that while the country was absorbed in the dramatic turmoil of high politics, these grassroots developments were quietly forming the foundation for a subsequent major transformation of the economy.

While the optimist can find some encouragement in this perspective, there is little prospect for a sharp resumption of the transition process in the next year or two. Among the principal reasons are the difficulty of dealing with the inflation and with the union-republic political conflict. The latter problem in particular has caused the sharp reversal in the process of political liberalization that Gorbachev has been leading in the last few months. This conservative reaction may well lead to a complete halt or even a reversal in the economic process of *perestroika*, although that is by no means foreordained. Should such a reversal occur, the old central planning system, perhaps somewhat modified, may gain a new lease on life. While it may endure for a period of time, however, there is no reason to expect that the restored planned economy would perform significantly better than it did in the past. A reaction of that sort would therefore only postpone the date on which some future General Secretary will be called on to lead a new effort at economic *perestroika*.

NOTES

1. U.S. Congress, Joint Economic Committee. *USSR: Measures of Economic Growth and Development, 1950-1980* (Washington: Government Printing Office, December 8, 1982), p. 20.

2. Among the pioneering works on the theory and measurement of factor productivity were Robert Solow, "Technical Change and the Aggregate Production Function," *Review of Economics and Statistics*, vol. 39, August 1957, pp. 312-320; and John Kendrick, *Productivity Trends in the United States* (Princeton: Princeton University Press, 1961). Among the first applications of factor productivity analysis to the Soviet economy were Joseph S. Berliner, "Static Efficiency of the Soviet Economy," *American Economic Review*, vol. 54, no. 3, May 1964, pp. 480-489; and Bela Balassa, "Dynamic Efficiency of the Soviet Economy," ibid. Sometime afterward, Soviet

economists began to apply the method to Soviet data. At the time it was politically awkward for Soviet economists to employ the methods of "bourgeois economics," so they invented the new terms "intensive" and "extensive" growth.

3. Abram Bergson. *Planning and Performance in Socialist Economies* (Boston: Unwin Hyman, 1989), pp. 13, 20. The coefficient of -.320 for the USSR is equivalent to output per worker 73 percent below that of the capitalist countries. The calculations are all made in U.S. prices. Because of the index number effect, if the calculations were made in the prices of the other country, Soviet output per worker would be somewhat lower.

Between 1975 and 1985, the rate of productivity growth declined in the major capitalist countries as well as in the USSR. The relative position of the USSR on the eve of Gorbachev's election may therefore have worsened somewhat but probably not significantly.

4. Because of the high rate of investment and of defense expenditures, the Soviet lag in relative *per capita* consumption was larger than the lag in labor productivity. Soviet *per capita* consumption was calculated to have been 42.5 percent that of the United States in 1976 when measured in U.S. prices, and 27.6 percent when measured in Soviet prices. Gertrude E. Schroeder, "Consumption," in Abram Bergson and Herbert S. Levine (eds.), *The Soviet Economy: Toward the Year 2000* (London: Allen and Unwin, 1983), p. 318.

5. Ronald Amman, Julian Cooper and R.W. Davies (eds.). *The Technological Level of Soviet Industry* (New Haven: Yale University Press, 1977), p. 66.

6. The following discussion is based on Anthony Jones and William Moskoff, *Ko-ops: The Rebirth of Entrepreneurship in the Soviet Union* (Bloomington: Indiana University Press, 1991).

7. James H. Noren. "The Soviet Economic Crisis: Another Perspective," *Soviet Economy,* vol. 6, January-March 1990, p. 27.

8. Philip Hanson. "Property Rights in the New Phase of Reforms," *Soviet Economy,* vol. 6, April-June 1990, pp. 111-118.

9. Marshall I. Goldman. "Gorbachev the Economist," *Foreign Affairs,* vol. 69, no. 2 (Spring) 1990, p. 39.

10. Foreign Broadcasting Information Service, SOV-90-102, 25 May 1990, p. 52.

11. Y. Chernisheva and M. Rozhkov, "The Beginnings of Producer Goods Auctions in the USSR," Berkeley-Duke Occasional Papers on the Second Economy in the USSR, Paper No. 22. September 1990.

12. Noren. "The Soviet Economic Crisis," p. 14.

13. In fact the production of consumer goods and services has not declined appreciably, nor has actual *per capita* consumption. The disorder in consumer goods markets caused by repressed inflation, however, has reduced the level of satisfaction derived from the given volume of real consumption. See Gertrude E. Schroeder, "'Crisis' in the Consumer Sector: A Comment," *Soviet Economy,* vol. 6, January-March 1990, pp. 62-63. Real consumption has also been redistributed from the poorer to the wealthier population who are able to pay the higher prices prevailing in the "second economy" and in other nonstate distribution channels.

14. Prime Minister Ryzhkov reported that food subsidies amounted to about 100 billion rubles in 1990. Foreign Broadcasting Information Service, ibid., p. 45.

15. *Pravda,* November 6, 1989, p. 11.

16. *The New York Times,* October 22, 1990, p. A6.

17. Dresser Industries of Dallas has been negotiating for four years on a proposal to build two oil equipment factories in the USSR. The negotiations have bogged down in a "tense tug-of-war

between Moscow and the republics" over who has the right to sign the contract. *The New York Times,* February 4, 1991, p. A1.

18. GNP has increased every year between 1985 and 1989. Preliminary results for 1990, however, suggest that production may have fallen last year. Noren, "The Soviet Economic Crisis," pp. 9, 40.

19. After a tense conflict over the size of the Russian republic contribution to the Union budget in 1991, an agreement was finally worked out. *The New York Times,* January 10, 1991.

Soviet Bureaucracy
and Economic Reform

Paul R. Gregory
University of Houston

Paper presented
November 14, 1990

Evolution in *Perestroika* Thinking

Gorbachev announced his intent in 1985 to introduce radical economic reform to the Soviet Union. He deliberately used the term "radical" to differentiate this reform from the half-hearted reforms of the past. The *perestroika* process has been running for over five years and has yielded few positive results.

The reform thinking of the Soviet leadership has evolved through three phases, although, it must be noted, the third phase is still in its infancy. Moreover, no one knows whether the Soviet Union will ever embark seriously on this third stage.

The first phase of *perestroika* dates to its first three to four years. This phase was characterized by naive expectations. It was thought that with relatively minor tinkering, the Soviet planned economy could be revived. A simple reduction in bureaucratic meddling plus the massive Western assistance that would be attracted by political liberalization would allow the Soviet economy to accelerate (*uskorenie*).

The second phase began in the 1988-1989 period, when it was clearly realized that minor tinkering would not yield the desired results. At this point, the leadership concluded that reform must go beyond minor repairs and deal with substantive issues. During this phase, it was determined to weaken the bureaucracy's hold on the economy and to unleash more local initiative. Although it was realized that fundamental legal, economic, and social reforms in laws and property rights were required, the argument was that these would take time, and that one must proceed with caution on introducing fundamental reform. However, it was felt that positive results would be achieved as a consequence of reducing the interventionary powers of the bureaucracy. During this phase, particular attention was devoted to the perceived problems of macroeconomic stability. Fundamental reforms could not be introduced prior to the introduction of stabilizing measures.

The third phase, which remained in its infancy in early 1991, began with the realization that reform requires dealing with the fundamental long-range issues. Institutions must be created that support market-like resource allocation. Property rights, freedom of and protection of contracts, and modern banking based upon commercial principles must be introduced. Although these issues have yet to be addressed concretely by official reform proposals, they are prominent in the reform packages put forward by the Yeltsin group—the 500-Day Program.

Issues of Bureaucratic Opposition

What exactly does the Soviet economic bureaucracy want from the reform process? What is the reform program of the bureaucracy? To a great extent, whether recognized or not, the interests of the bureaucracy have been reflected in the reform program of the Ryzhkov and Pavlov governments. The bureaucratic attitude towards reform can be characterized by the following propositions.

(1) The economy is not yet ready for markets for a variety of reasons, the most prominent being macroeconomic imbalances.

(2) Reform is inevitably a slow process in which substantive reforms must be introduced gradually.

(3) The costs of rapid reform are too substantial. Reform must be introduced gradually to limit the social costs.

Why do bureaucrats oppose substantive economic reform? A number of reasons can be suggested, both valid and invalid.

First, they realize that true economic reform means a loss of jobs and a reduction in authority and prestige. The reform discussion has already made them pariahs in their communities.

Second, economic reform is truly a power struggle, a struggle over who controls economic resources: Who will control diamonds, or oil, or building permits? These decisions determine who has the power in society.

Third, among the bureaucracy there is a sincere feeling that the economy will collapse without centralized directives. Planners and bureaucrats have an ingrained physical balance mentality that causes them to fear market allocation. They simply cannot perceive how it could work. To Soviet bureaucrats, "deficits" are inherent to the economy. They can only be removed by administrative measures, not by prices.

Although it is generally perceived that Soviet managers form the natural constituency for radical reform, this is far from the case. There is a true ambiguity of managerial attitudes towards reform. Experienced managers have developed a comfort level with the old system. They understand that the transition period will be rocky. Moreover, the outcome of reform is by no means certain. Managers understand that a half-way reform would likely leave them worse off. Attitudes towards reform vary depending upon whether managers will have ready markets for their goods both at home and in the West after the marketization has taken place. It is noteworthy that the major organized opposition to reform from the ranks of managers has come from directors of heavy-industrial establishments.

Bureaucratic Excuses

Bureaucrats put forward a number of reasons for delaying substantive reforms and continuing to rely on minor tinkering.

First, bureaucrats cite the specter of inflation. Because Soviet prices have for decades been kept at artificially low levels, especially retail prices, conversion to market resource allocation would mean substantial increases in prices.

It is interesting to note the emphasis placed on fear of inflation in the Soviet Union. Lenin had described inflation as the instrument that can destroy capitalism, and this thinking has caused Soviet authorities to have a perhaps irrational fear of inflation, which is shared by the population. Soviet bureaucrats and authorities confuse the income redistribution effects of inflation with the inefficiency effects of inflation. It is clear that a move to clearing prices will have strong income redistributing effects, and that measures to protect those on fixed incomes must be put in place. The move to clearing prices, as long as it does not lead to hyperinflation, however, should have a positive effect on efficiency. People and managers will, for the first time, make resource allocation decisions based on relative scarcities. Economic theory has taught that moderate inflation, if properly anticipated, does not affect real output and hence efficiency.

Second, Soviet bureaucrats use the specter of monopoly as an excuse for not moving into the third phase of reform. The administrative-command economy has, over the years, created a highly concentrated industrial structure with individual suppliers having significant market power. Bureaucrats argue that one cannot use market allocation with such high levels of concentration. Planners must use their control of investment decisions to create a system of alternate suppliers before moving to market allocation.

The process of creating alternate suppliers will be, at best, slow and gradual. Moreover, it seems unrealistic to rely on the planning structure—which created the monopoly problem in the first place—to create an optimal industrial structure. Bureaucrats do not understand the notion that free entry under conditions of market allocation is a more reliable way to resolve the monopoly problem even though they recognize that state pricing rules can be used to limit monopoly profits during the transition period.

Third, Soviet bureaucrats contend that opening the Soviet economy will have disastrous consequences unless foreign transactions remain under the center's strict control. Such concerns are not unusual in a country with limited foreign exchange earnings and growing hard currency debt. Other bureaucratic concerns about opening the economy are less standard. Soviet foreign trade bureaucrats believe that only "rich" economies can gain from trade. If the Soviet economy enters the international trade arena as a "poor" economy, it will prove uncompetitive. This type of thinking ignores the fact that comparative advantage allows both rich and poor countries to benefit from trade, if they specialize according to comparative advantage. The corollary of this thinking is the belief that the Soviet economy must first become "wealthy" before it can effectively trade with the West. Insofar as this "wealth" is a long way off, liberalizing foreign trade must be delayed.

Another nonstandard reason for delaying trade liberalization is the fear that valuable Soviet resources will be lost. Given the distorted domestic pricing system, unscrupulous Westerners will take advantage of pricing "mistakes" in both Soviet products and assets. These pricing mistakes will allow the Western world to acquire Soviet products and assets at unreasonably low prices.

The fear of Western exploitation reflects bureaucratic attitudes towards pricing. The Soviet bureaucrat views prices as instruments to be controlled by higher authority; under this system, prices do not change frequently. Even if pricing officials see that particular Soviet products and assets are being bought by Westerners at alarming rates, they would not be able to use these pricing signals quickly enough to raise prices to prevent the exploitation from taking place. Rather than viewing Western purchases as a means of obtaining valuable information on scarcity prices, Soviet pricing officials view Western purchases as a destabilizing threat. Similar fears, for example, prompted high Soviet officials in early 1991 to warn of Western banking conspiracies aimed to buying valuable Soviet products and assets at bargain-basement prices.

Chaos and the Command Economy

There has been a substantial dismantling of the Soviet economic bureaucracy. Staff cuts in Moscow bureaucratic organizations have averaged 30 percent; the industrial ministries—organizations that provided the glue that held the command system together—have been hard hit. Industrial enterprises no longer answer to the local party secretary. It is unclear who can make and enforce decisions in today's Soviet economy. The balance of power has begun to shift towards the enterprise and away from the state committees, industrial ministries, and local party officials. Enterprises no longer automatically fulfill directives from above.

Restrictions of enterprise autonomy remain most prominent in those areas most essential to marketization of the Soviet economy. Enterprises still are not free to set their own prices, acquire their own supplies, and complete deals with Western companies. Pricing officials continue to insist on cost-based pricing formulae that do not reflect demand and that "protect" the public from excess profits. Industrial managers must sell deficit products at state-dictated prices that often provide little or no profit. Few Soviet bureaucrats want wholesale trade to replace centralized distribution, even though this is a declared goal of *perestroika*. In fact, most feel that wholesale trade would worsen rather than help the troubled material-technical supply system, which remains the weakest point in the Soviet system.

What reform package would Soviet economic bureaucrats be willing to support? They would like to see an economic system in which roughly half of enterprise output is dictated by state orders. The centralized supply system would be retained, with enterprises allowed to deal only at the margin in products produced above quotas. Less than one-quarter of Moscow bureaucrats favor giving enterprises freedom to set their own prices. The bureaucratic "reform" package falls far short even of the modest official proposals of the late 1980s. The stereotype of bureaucratic opposition to radical reform is accurate. In a society that has traditionally rewarded bureaucrats for agreeing with the official line ("*perestroika* will be a success"), it is remarkable that less than half of Moscow bureaucrats feel that *perestroika* will eventually be successful.

The clear-cut identification of enterprise managers as the major beneficiaries of reform conceals an interesting ambiguity. Managers fear a move away from key features of the old system. The enterprise manager's fear of the unknown is understandable. In a chaotic system that mixes command and market elements, that assigns arbitrary prices, taxes away excess profits, and fails to assign clear property rights, who can predict whether the experienced manager's lot will be improved? Soviet managers would obviously prefer a well-functioning market system if presented a choice. Enough of them have seen it at work in Western Europe, Japan, and the United States. Managerial support for the more comfortable aspects of the old system reflects the lack of faith in the ability of the Soviet leadership to devise a nonchaotic system that combines market and plan.

Neither the Soviet bureaucrat nor the enterprise manager appears to understand how a market economy works. Sixty years of command system have taught both groups to think in terms of administrative balancing of supplies and demand. Goods are inherently in deficit. Shortages can only be eliminated by producing more. Raising the price has nothing to do with the "deficitness" of the commodity. Soviet bureaucrats believe in the visible hand of administrative methods. They openly worry about where the wheat, steel, shoes, and cigarettes will come from if they are not planned from above. In addition to personal concerns for their jobs and livelihood, Soviet bureaucrats are convinced that the economy could not continue to function in an orderly manner without them.

The limited economic reform that has taken place appears to have made things worse, as evidenced by declining growth, supply crises, hoarding, strikes, and rising inflation. The explanation is quite simple: *Perestroika* has dismantled much of the Soviet command system prior to establishing a new market order. The chaos associated with the erosion of the planned order threatens public and official support for radical reform. The Soviet public and the Soviet leadership may associate chaos with market reform rather than with the collapse of the command system. Moreover, the fear of the chaos inherent in a partial reform, could deprive the reform movement of its natural constituents, the industrial managers.

Can "command" be restored to an economy that has experienced the first steps of decentralization? Both enterprise managers and Moscow bureaucrats agree that local party influence over the economy has largely disappeared. They agree that the influence of industrial ministries and state committees has fallen considerably. Managers now pick and choose the directives they are prepared to implement. *Ad hoc* decisionmaking has replaced the old rules and regulations of the administrative-command economy.

We return to the issue of the optimal phasing of reform. The phasing chosen by the Soviet leadership has, obviously, not been successful. The Soviet leadership has chosen, as a first step, to dismantle significant elements of the command apparatus (most particularly the ministry command system) and to give enterprises new but restricted freedoms. Moreover, the local party command element has largely disappeared. The glue that once held the command system together has disappeared, and a new form of glue has yet to be put in place—namely, the discipline of the market.

The Soviet economy finds itself lacking disciplinary forces, either from the side of command or from the side of markets. The monetary control system that was previously based upon strict governmental and political control of monetary emissions has dissipated into an ineffective system designed to win political allies. Strict wage increase formulae (wages should not increase more rapidly than productivity) have been laid aside. Enterprises, with strengthened workers' collectives now set their own wage increases, still without a hard budget constraint. The central budget is in chaos because of the failure to resolve center-republic relations, and budget deficits must be covered by printing money. Strikes represent a thorny problem because market forces are not providing information on which wage requests to grant and which to deny.

These events cause one to question whether a cautious, phased reform will work. Moreover, it threatens loss of political support for reform. The "cold turkey" approach, judging by the Polish experience, causes substantial output declines and a substantial upward movement in prices in the reform's first phase. However, under the cold turkey approach, the eventual benefits should be felt in the relatively near future. This sense may allow public support for reform to endure the difficult first phase. Under the Soviet gradualist approach, a slow hemorrhage becomes a faster hemorrhage, and there is no end in sight to the problem. To expect public support for reform to continue in this environment is unrealistic.

Soviet Economic Reform
The Transition Problem

Herbert S. Levine
University of Pennsylvania

Paper presented
March 13, 1991

The Basic Difficulty Facing the Soviet Economy

The fundamental issue facing Soviet economic reform today is the problem of transition from a centralized to a decentralized economic system. Even if the design for a new economic mechanism were perfect, the dominant problem would still be: how do you get there from here. This paper will focus on the issue of transition—its meaning and its consequences for the progress of Soviet economic reform.

It is important to note from the start that while there is abundant Western theory to help Soviet economists design a market system, there is no available theory of transition from a centralized arrangement of economic institutions to a decentralized one. Western economists have not been concerned with this issue, since the development of decentralized economic mechanisms in the West took place slowly over long periods of time spanning more than a century. And Soviet economists themselves have only recently begun to work on the issue. Previously it was not a subject of concern, since radical market-type reform itself was not openly discussed. Hence there are no theoretical guides, either Western or Soviet, that Soviet leaders and economists can draw upon as they attempt to deal with the problems of transition.

At the base of the transition problem is the interrelated nature of an economic system. One element of the system cannot be changed without changing other elements if true change in economic behavior is to be achieved. Thus, to give Soviet managers decisionmaking power over what they are to produce, they must also be given the power to decide what inputs they will use: materials, labor, and machinery.

First, if managers are to have the power to decide what materials they will use, the centralized system of material supply, introduced in the 1930s, has to be abolished and a system of wholesale trade put in its place. But given the widespread nature of material shortages in Soviet industry, there is a fear that the removal of the centralized materials rationing system will exacerbate these shortages and cause massive disequilibria in the economy. Supporters of reform, however, argue that the rationing system itself contributes to the appearance of shortages, because managers, operating within the administrative centralized supply system, order an excessive amount of inputs to protect themselves against the inefficiencies and uncertainties of the command system.

Second, Soviet managers have to be given increased power over the hiring and firing of workers. If managers are to be encouraged to seek out and adopt advanced technology in the pursuit of the reform's goal of economic modernization, they have to have the right to adjust their labor force to the quantity and quality levels appropriate to the new technology. This means giving managers the right not only to fire workers who are malingering, but also those who are working hard but who are made redundant by the new technology. Thus the extensive job security enjoyed by Soviet workers, especially during the Brezhnev period, will be diminished. But as many Soviet economists argue, the Soviet guarantee of full employment should guarantee the Soviet worker *a* job, not guarantee *his* job. Institutional arrangements will have to be expanded for handling unemployment and for the retraining and redistribution of labor.

Third, managers have to have the power to acquire the capital equipment that they decide they need. This again involves the abolition of the centralized system of materials and equipment supply and its replacement with a market system of wholesale trade. It also involves the question of investment and credit. If managers are to have the power to acquire capital equipment on their own, then they have to have access to the financial means to acquire this equipment. More-over, to maintain the goal of decentralization, the banking institutions that decide on the allocation of investment credit must also be decentralized and should make their decisions upon the commercial credit-worthiness of loan applicants rather than on any centralized investment plan.

If this freedom for Soviet managers to acquire the inputs they decide they need is not to lead to rampant inflation, their demands must be constrained. With the removal of centralized control over supplies and labor, the constraint that must be instituted is a hard budget constraint. That is, managers must be required to cover the cost of their inputs out of the revenues they earn. If they fail to do so, the process of bank-ruptcy must be enforced. Without the vulnerability to bankruptcy, the freeing-up of managerial decisionmaking will not work.

Furthermore, if managers are to make their own output and input decisions, independent of central planners, they will need meaningful signals with regard to economic costs and benefits so that the pursuit of profit will lead to the efficient use of resources. Otherwise, decentralized decisionmaking will lead to substantial inefficiency and waste. This means the Soviet price system will have to undergo radical reform. Not only will subsidies have to be removed, but the system for setting prices will have to be changed. Buyers and sellers must be given the right to negotiate their own prices in a free and flexible way so that prices adequately reflect the conditions of supply and demand in the economy.

The reform of the Soviet economy is, in essence, a monetization of economic transactions and decisionmaking. The target planning of the command system is to be replaced by producer and user decisionmaking involving magnitudes calibrated in monetary terms. Therefore, monetary stability becomes critical. Issues of macroeconomic policy and control—the size of the money supply and of the government deficit—become of great importance. If the required monetary control is not exercised and if reasonable monetary stability is not achieved and maintained before and along with the introduction of the reforms, then the resulting surge of inflation will seriously weaken or destroy the effectiveness of the reform.

Finally, the reforms described so far may not work in the absence of one further element, namely, competition. Without the introduction of competition, without buyers being given a choice among competing suppliers, decentralization may not lead to the meeting of customer demands, efficiency, and technological dynamism, but to monopoly and the danger of continued technological stagnation and price inflation. Therefore, an additional element of the required set of reforms may be the introduction of a Soviet antitrust policy.

What all of this means is that due to the interrelatedness of an economic system, a number of reforms must be introduced more or less simultaneously in order for economic reform to begin to have any effect. In other words, to get the rocket of economic reform off the launching pad, an initial bundle of simultaneous reforms is required. One of the aims of an economic theory and policy of transition should be the pursuit of "minimum simultaneity," i.e., the development of a minimum bundle of simultaneous reforms required to launch the economic reform. For if everything has to be done at once, then the introduction of a decentralizing reform would face overwhelming obstacles. Especially under conditions of extensive market disequilibria, an abrupt shift from a centralized system to a full price-profit-market-money system would produce chaos.

In the elaboration of a theory of transition, it is necessary that the destabilization produced by the introduction of institutional changes be constrained to a level that allows the economy to continue to function. Certainly this is a policy constraint demanded by political leaders. Officials at Gosplan and the economic ministries are criticized for continuing to operate in the old ways. But at the same time, they are held responsible for the performance of the economy. The only way these officials know how to carry out this responsibility is by means of the old planning and control methods.

The key problem here is that the leaders want reform, but they want to bring it about without acutely destabilizing the economy. The maintenance of some of the old forms of planning and control is necessary to prevent destabilization. Thus, the transition process initially involves the introduction of new forms alongside the old forms, rather than immediately in place of them, with the idea that the new forms are to grow and in time replace the old forms. This growth and replacement process is, however, not well understood. To what extent does the maintenance of old forms inhibit, or even prevent, the development and growth of new forms, and what is the nature of the replacement process if it does take place?

There is, in addition, another underlying tension in the politics-economics relationship. An effective economic mechanism is one that produces rapid adjustment to changing conditions, to changes in technology and changes in people's desires. But adjustment involves the pain of dislocation. It reduces people's security. It affects rewards and penalties and the distribution of income. A socialist system politicizes the allocation of pain. A capitalist market system tends to depoliticize it. Though people in all countries look to their governments for protection against pain, in socialist countries this feeling is particularly strong. Thus there is the danger that the political pressure for government protection and intervention will prevent the economy from adequately adjusting to change, thus inhibiting the progress of economic reform or limiting its effectiveness.

The Record of Reform

When Gorbachev came to power in March 1985, his initial economic program was focused on the re-invigoration, rather than the reform, of the economy. Gorbachev called for growth acceleration and economic modernization based upon sharp increases in investment directed toward machine building and energy, plus extensive changes in administrative and management personnel. It was not until June 1987 that discussion of serious economic reform began. At a meeting of the Central Committee of the Soviet Communist Party, a resolution calling for the radical restructuring of the Soviet economy was adopted. The resolution recognized that the interrelatedness of an economic system required a bundle of changes to be made for any real change in the functioning of the economy to result. It did not, however, appear to recognize the difficulties of transition that would be involved.

The June 1987 resolution was accompanied by a new law on the state enterprise. Together they formed a program which promised a substantial move toward economic decentralization. The program called for the virtual abolition of the annual state plan and its obligatory targets, significant independence of enterprise managers from control by the center and the industrial ministries, enterprise incentives based on the pursuit of profit and financial responsibility, flexibility in the payment and allocation of labor, and reform of prices and the system of price formation. The new system was to be in place by the beginning of the 1990s. Until then, some aspects of centralization were to be retained, e.g., the so-called "state production orders," which were obligatory for the enterprises to fulfill.

A year later, in June 1988, Gorbachev launched a radical political reform affecting both central and local governments. An elected congress of people's deputies was created, which in turn elected a president and a legislative parliament (Supreme Soviet). And local councils (soviets) were to be directly elected by the people. Gorbachev appears to have concluded that political reform is a necessary precondition for economic reform. In order for economic reform to succeed, decision-makers must have the information they need to make decisions, and they must be free of arbitrary government intervention in carrying out their decisions. Leaders in government and in the economy must be accountable for the results of the actions they take. They must have credibility in the eyes of the people. Thus, *glasnost* and democratization are prerequisites for successful economic reform.

What can be said about the accomplishments of radical economic reform so far since its launching at the June 1987 meeting of the Central Committee of the Soviet Communist party? Clearly, little progress has been made. The reform is barely off the launching pad. And there are a number of highly serious and troublesome developments, in particular the growth of inflationary forces, the spreading shortages of consumer goods, and the recent decreasing levels of output. Indeed, a thick cloud of crisis hangs over the economy and the people's expectations for the future are bleak.

Among the major causes of the present situation, it can be argued, is first of all an initial lack of sufficient understanding and appreciation by Soviet economists and leaders of the macroeconomic factors involved in the transition to a decentralized economic mechanism. Wage inflation (and through it, price inflation) has been a direct function of money creation resulting from (1) the government deficit, which has been substantial (even when account is taken of the fact that in the Soviet Union most of the investment in the economy is on the government budget), and (2) enterprise managers' pressure to increase money wages far beyond increases in productivity, given the flexibility of the incentive wage system accompanying the reform. Much of the current problem of empty shelves and consumer goods shortages is demand-related, that is, a consequence of the sizable increases in money wages which would not have been possible except for the action of the printing presses bloating the supply of money and the growth of the monetary overhang in the economy.

There has also, however, been a slowdown in the growth of output. This has been a result of the fact that, while some of the glue of the old administrative-command methods of management that held the economy together has been removed, and new economic methods of management have not developed fast enough to replace it. The first element of the economic mechanism to be affected has been that of interenterprise flows of materials. The coordination mechanism in the economy has been seriously weakened leading to a slowing down of growth and, this year, an actual decrease in output.

A further critical flaw has been the failure to introduce price reform. The maintenance of below-market-clearing prices, often through the payment of subsidies, contributes to the government deficit and to the prevalence of goods shortages. And the maintenance of the centralized system of price setting means that prices are not flexible signals of the relationship between supply and demand.

Thus the simultaneity problem in the transition to a decentralized economic system has proved to be a formidable barrier to the progress of Soviet economic reform.

In light of the failure of economic reform to get started and the growing sense of crisis in the country, several important developments have occurred with regard both to increased understanding of the economic issues and the working out of proposed programs for economic reform, particularly for the handling of the issue of transition.

First there has been a growing understanding among Soviet economists of the principles and importance of macroeconomic policies. Fiscal and monetary policies are discussed in a clear and straightforward manner, with the stress placed on the role they will play in the reformed Soviet market economy, particularly their role in managing inflation. Much attention in the public discussion of economic reform has been given to the monetary overhang and to ways of stopping its growth and of decreasing it: taxing excessive increase in money wages, and sale of shares, bonds, and apartments to the public.

Another important development in economic discussions over the past year has been the increasing focus on property rights and the creation of new diverse nonstate property relations. "Destatization" has become a rallying cry. What is of great importance here is the growing perception that a profit incentive is not enough to give an enterprise manager the needed sense of responsibility for the economic assets under his control. An ownership relationship is also necessary. Ownership brings with it not only an interest in an increase in the flow of profit (income) but also an interest in an increase in the value of the property (wealth), which leads to the protection and nurturing of society's assets.

In addition to the progress in understanding economic issues, there have been two or three major programs for economic reform put forth in the last year, each with a strong focus on the transition issue.

First, there was a report issued in October 1989 by the State Commission on Economic Reform headed by the economist Abalkin, a Deputy Prime Minister in the Ryzhkov government. The report outlines a design for a future Soviet market economy and discusses in some detail the measures to be taken to move the Soviet economy through the transition from a centralized structure to a future decentralized market structure.

The vision of a reformed Soviet economy spelled out in the report goes far beyond that proposed in the resolution of June 1987. While that resolution was ambiguous about the extent to which the new system would be a market economy, the Abalkin report unambiguously envisions a market economy. It states that, on the basis of Soviet experience, there clearly is no reliable alternative to a market mechanism as a means of coordinating the action and interests of economic units. It goes on to state that the market is also the most democratic form of regulating economic activity. The Abalkin report makes clear that a market system contains an array of markets. In addition to goods markets (for both consumer goods and producer goods), it includes financial markets (markets for securities and a stock market) and labor markets.

The report stresses that in the reformed economy there will be many forms of property ownership: leasing and cooperatives, farmer and peasant property, joint-stock companies, corporations, joint-ventures, and private property (though private individual property will not be permitted to lead to the "exploitation of man by man"). The report also declares that the state should transfer the administration of the economic property that it retains to the workers' collectives on the basis of lease contracts.

According to the report, the financial sector, fiscal and monetary and banking institutions, should be thoroughly developed. And the state should exercise its influence on the economy through a wide assortment of economic means, fiscal and monetary policies, rather than administrative controls.

Finally, extensive attention is paid in the design of the reformed economy and (elsewhere in the report) to social guarantees for all members of society, including those with few skills.

A major part of the report is devoted to the issue of transition. Three possible approaches are discussed. What are termed the conservative and radical approaches are dismissed, the first because it will never produce any progress in reform and the second because it will lead to chaos. What is called the "radical-moderate" approach is the one preferred. In essence it is a step-by-step approach for preparing and then introducing a bundle of simultaneous reforms which include a well-developed set of government fiscal and monetary controls. These will be used to manage the inflation which is inevitable with the introduction of markets in an environment of shortages. Extensive attention in the report is also paid to the protection of the people in light of the painful adjustments required. This protection will help people adapt to a market system. Included here is the indexation of incomes and pensions. It is clearly aimed at reviving popular support for the economic reform and the movement to the market.

The report also sketches out a schedule for the transition to the reformed economic system. Four stages are described covering the periods 1990, 1991-1992, 1993-1995, and 1996-2000, by the end of which a new economic system will be established.

The report was discussed at a large conference of economists in November, where it was criticized from both the right and the left. Conservatives attacked the conversion of the Soviet economy to a market economy. And the radicals attacked what they considered to be the excessive protection of workers from the economic adjustments which they argued were necessary for the success of economic reform, i.e., the creation of a flexible, efficient, responsive economic mechanism.

In December, Prime Minister Ryzhkov stated that he supported the Abalkin program, but called for a two-year delay in its introduction, during which heavy centralized priority would be put on increasing the production of consumer goods to eradicate consumer shortages. This echo of the administrative-command approach was not well received. It was followed in May 1990 by a formal government plan put forth by Ryzhkov that was similar in some ways to the Abalkin program, but it called for beginning the transition to a market economy with an immediate (July 1990) doubling of basic food prices, coupled with indexing of wages and pensions. This was rejected by the Soviet parliament, and Ryzhkov and Abalkin were instructed to return in September with a revised program.

In the interim, dramatic changes were taking place in the Soviet political scene. Power was shifting from the Communist Party to the elected government bodies and from the Kremlin to the republics. In April 1990, Boris Yeltsin was elected president of the Russian republic. He made clear his intentions to assert Russian republic sovereignty over the economy of the Russian republic, and his intention to move the republic quickly—in 500 days—to a market economy. At the end of the Soviet Communist party congress in July, Yeltsin left the party, strengthening his position as an independent political force.

Gorbachev thus faced a serious challenge, particularly sharp in the economic sector. He responded with a compromising approach. A joint Gorbachev-Yeltsin working group was set up at the end of July, under the direction of the respected economist Shatalin, a member of Gorbachev's Presidential Council, with the task of drawing up a program for the transition to a market economy. The working group met during the month of August and at the beginning of September submitted a lengthy report, including drafts of over 20 laws, which comprised a program for the transition to a market economy in 500 days.

The essence of the Shatalin transition program was quite different from that of Ryzhkov and Abalkin. The heart of the program lay in the rapidity of the transition process, in the dominant role it gave to privatization and to stabilization, and in its recognition of the sovereignty of the republics as the foundation for the creation of an economic union.

The rapidity of the transition process was symbolized by the phrase "500 days." This timeframe was not to be taken literally, but it represented a commitment to move ahead resolutely with a tightly sequenced bundle of reforms, recognizing the simultaneity problem. Such a commitment was critical in establishing the credibility of the reform program, which in turn was so important for the program's success. Furthermore, the Shatalin group made clear that they were talking about the transition to a market system, not the full development of such a system. The latter, it was generally acknowledged, would take several decades.

Second, the transition to the market was to be built on the basis of privatization rather than on the decentralization of state enterprise management. Privatization was to proceed from the top (turning state enterprises into joint-stock companies) and from the bottom (helping private people to set up small and medium-sized firms, with credit and access to space and materials). Financial institutions necessary for privatization (stock markets, commodity exchanges, etc.) were to be set up.

Third, stabilization policies were to be introduced immediately. Investment financed through the state budget was to be cut sharply as were the defense and KGB budgets. Tight monetary policy was to be initiated. Monetary reform through confiscation was to be avoided. Rather, the monetary overhang was to be absorbed through the increased supply of consumer goods (production and imports) and sales to the public of apartments and a range of state assets. The prices of up to 150 basic consumer goods were to remain fixed for the entire period of one-and-one-half years. Reform of other prices was to start as soon as the stabilization program began to take hold.

The aim of the stabilization program was to make the ruble the accepted, totally fungible, legal tender throughout the Soviet Union. As some members of the Shatalin group put it, the aim was to make the ruble "real money."

The fourth key element in the approach of the Shatalin program was that it started with the recognition of the sovereignty of the republics, and it tried to create institutional arrangements that would encourage the republics to give up some of their sovereignty in order to share in the benefits of these arrangements. A good example of such an institution was the proposed central bank, which was designed along the lines of the American Federal Reserve System. The board of governors of the bank consisted of a chairman and representatives from each of the republics. Thus each republic that joined the system would have a voice in the setting of monetary policy for the entire economic union.

The battleground is now in the political arena. As the old economic, social, and political structures are being destroyed, and new structures are slow in developing, instability is increasing. To deal with the situation, it is necessary for Soviet political leaders, primarily Gorbachev and Yeltsin, to reach certain agreements. First, they must agree on the nature of the new Soviet political union and the level of sovereignty of the republics. Without this, the political power to implement economic reform is lost. And second, they must agree on a program of economic reform, one that addresses the major problems of transition—"minimum simultaneity," property rights, and macroeconomic balance. Two different approaches have already been proposed and more are possible. If they come to an agreement soon, then there is a chance that by the turn of the century the Soviet economy will look substantially different from what it was and is today, and will begin to show signs of becoming a market economy with economic, financial, and legal institutions resembling those of the advanced industrial nations.

If, on the other hand, there is great delay in the political acceptance and introduction of significant transition measures, then the disequilibria and instability in the economy will intensify and the reimposition of economic controls will be likely. Where this path will lead is not clear. It can be argued, however, that since recentralization will not solve the problems facing the Soviet economy, another cycle of economic reform will be initiated in five to ten years. In *perestroika* II, Soviet leaders and the Soviet people, with the experience they have gained, may be more successful in dealing with economic reform and its transition problems, and a Soviet market economy may begin to take shape toward the end of the first decade of the twenty-first century.

The Economic Transformation of Eastern Europe

Josef C. Brada
Arizona State University

Paper presented
January 23, 1991

The countries of Eastern Europe, and particularly the more developed ones—Czechoslovakia, Hungary and Poland—are undergoing three distinct but interrelated processes. The first is the process of transition, whereby the system of central planning and the ideologically-based primacy of social ownership of capital is replaced by a system where markets and market-based allocations of resources play a primacy role and where private ownership of the means of production assumes a significant, if not at first predominant, role. In the long run, the success of this transition is the critical economic issue for the region. Short-term changes in output or economic welfare cannot mask either the shortcomings of the old economic system or the potential inherent in the market system. Nevertheless, the potential that markets and private property hold for the economic future of Eastern Europe will not be realized quickly or easily. A measure of economic knowledge, wise governance, and policymaking and a political system that can maintain a balance between responsiveness to the popular will and political expediency are the least that will be needed.

The second economic process going on in Eastern Europe involves managing the short-term macroeconomic shocks to which the region is subject. Framing the proper responses to these shocks is first, for the

NOTE: The author is indebted to the Bundesinstitut fur ostwissenschaftliche und internationale Studien in Koln for providing a productive working environment for the writing of this paper and to their fellowship program, sponsored by the Volkswagen Stiftung, for financial support.

rejection of Communism had much to do with its economic failures. Thus today's governments in Eastern Europe face a legacy of deteriorating economic conditions.

In Czechoslovakia and Hungary the past decade has yielded stagnant or deteriorating incomes, while in Poland the worsening of economic performance has been, as Table 1 shows, more precipitous. Less easy to quantify but equally serious has been the worsening environmental degradation of the region, the extent of which is evident even to the casual visitor and the effects of which have resulted in a dramatic decline in health for the region's populations. To these long-term trends are now added inflation and unemployment. Having put up with the empty economic promises of the Communist regimes for over 40 years, and having experienced declining living standards for the past 10 to 15 years people in these countries are impatient for palpable signs of economic progress. It is unlikely that they are willing to accept long-term solutions that call for greater sacrifice today in return for promises of a better, but distant, future. Thus, governments in the region have only a limited amount of political capital and limited room to maneuver. Policymakers must seek to produce concrete and visible gains in the short run without adopting policies that are expedient or simply benefit politically powerful groups at the expense of appropriate long-run policies.

The third process is one of rejoining the world economy. The pattern of trade that emerged in the Communist era, emphasizing the role of the Soviet Union as the major trade partner of the Eastern European countries and, perhaps more perniciously, limiting economic competition from and with market economies, was a major source of the economic shortcomings of the Eastern European economies. Thus, a redirection of trade toward the West offers both an injection of modern technology and know-how, as well as of competition and economic rationality that should benefit the countries of Eastern Europe. Unfortunately, the potential benefits of this turn toward the West are being outweighed by the negative consequences of its abrupt and partly involuntary nature, which is the result of the collapse of the Soviet economy and of the Council for Mutual Economic Assistance

(CMEA), the organization that facilitated trade among these countries. This collapse of trade has led both to a more drastic shift in trade patterns and to a greater decline in the volume of trade of these countries than was desired. Moreover, the shift toward the West has occurred at a time when western economic growth has slowed, thus diminishing the short-term capacity of world markets to absorb the exports of Eastern Europe.

Table 1
Changes in Net Material Product in Czechoslovakia,
Hungary, and Poland, 1979-1989

Year	Percent Change in Net Material Product in:		
	Czechoslovakia	Hungary	Poland
1979	3.1	1.2	-2.3
1980	2.9	-0.9	-6.0
1981	-0.1	2.5	-12.0
1982	0.2	2.6	-5.5
1983	2.3	0.3	6.0
1984	3.5	2.5	5.6
1985	3.0	-1.4	3.4
1986	2.6	0.9	4.9
1987	2.1	4.1	1.9
1988	2.4	0.3	4.9
1989	1.3	-2.0	0.3

SOURCE: United Nations Economic Commission for Europe, *Economic Survey of Europe in 1989-1990*. New York: United Nations, 1990.

These three processes interact with each other, often in ways that seem unpredictable to policymakers and that are not clearly understood by the population. Thus, if we are to have a clear view of Eastern Europe's current economic situation and a realistic appraisal of its future prospects, we need to disentangle the processes in order to understand how they are likely to influence Eastern Europe's economic future.

The Economics and Politics of Transition

A transition from a socialist, centrally planned economy to a capitalist, market-oriented one requires the creation of markets and of the institutions that support and facilitate market processes; the privatization or at least "de-etatization" of productive capital; and the creation of a set of mechanisms that will allow the government to maintain control over macroeconomic aggregates and to provide an appropriate level of public services without interfering excessively with microeconomic processes in the economy.

The Conceptual Issues of Creating Markets

One difficulty with creating markets is that freeing prices tends to create inflation, which may cause social backlash against reform or unleash an inflationary spiral that would destroy markets. In some countries, such as pre-1989 Poland, there was a severe macroeconomic disequilibrium, characterized by large cash holdings among the population, a shortage of goods at existing and artificially low prices, and a large government deficit that continued to fuel the growth of the money supply. Even in countries such as Czechoslovakia and Hungary where there was less of an imbalance between the demand for and the supply of goods, the existing pattern of prices was badly distorted. Prices of food, housing, and energy were too low, largely the result of consumption and production subsidies.

Thus, the liberalization of prices would have two effects. The first would be to increase the general price level so as to reflect the existing monetary overhang. While such an increase, if matched by equal increases in real wages, acts largely to reduce the value of cash hoards, it nevertheless has important implications for the distribution of income because older or wealthier individuals, who have a greater stock of savings, lose at the expense of younger or poorer individuals. At the same time, it is not possible to tie all incomes to the price level, and thus pensioners and public servants, whose incomes are relatively inflexible in nominal terms, tend to be obvious victims of such a general price increase. The latter groups, along with other low-income individuals, are also especially vulnerable to the second effect of price liberalization, the change in relative prices that operates largely to raise the price of highly subsidized necessities such as food, clothing, and shelter. Since such goods make up a very large share of the budget of low-income consumers, price reform is seen as causing large and, from the standpoint of social justice, unacceptable changes in the distribution of income. Indeed, to the extent that the former low prices of consumer goods were maintained by a combination of shortages, subsidies, and low wages, raising prices to unsubsidized market levels can be seen as replacing an invisible system of taxes with one that is visible and thus more unpopular.

Changes in prices will also alter the financial fortunes of many firms and of the workers employed by them. However, there are as yet no clear provisions for bankruptcy. It is true that laws on bankruptcy have been enacted in most Eastern European countries, but there have been few or no bankruptcies. In part, this is due to a misunderstanding of managerial incentives for declaring bankruptcy. Specifically, the Eastern European bankruptcy legislation implicitly assumes that it will be the managers of loss-making firms who will declare their firms bankrupt. However, both to retain their jobs and because of unfailing human optimism, it is not the managers of loss-making firms who opt for bankruptcy, either in western market economies or in Eastern Europe. Instead, it is the creditors of the failing firm who force the bankruptcy, largely in an effort to obtain some part of the equity in the failing firm, so as to secure the loans they have made to the firm. Unfortunately, Eastern European enterprises, like the majority of state-owned firms in other countries, lack equity; they are financed largely by debt, and consequently bankruptcy provides little prospect to creditors of obtaining assets that can cover any significant portion of their loans to the failing firm. Thus, like the managers of the failing firms, banks and other creditors are forced to rely on optimism and to hope that debtor firms can return to profitability. As a consequence, the structure of production fails to adjust to price signals as rapidly as it should while, at the same time, the financial system is increasingly undermined by the accumulated debt of unprofitable firms.

Finally, the creation of markets requires the creation of institutions such as commodities and stock exchanges and the enactment of business and commercial laws. The complex task of creating this institutional and legal infrastructure entails both conceptual and practical difficulties. On the one hand, it is argued that the most modern institutional arrangements available in the West, and particularly in the European Community (EC), with which many Eastern European countries wish to align themselves, should be introduced as quickly as possible. The argument for this strategy is that it will provide institutions which, because of their modernity, will last a long time and provide a stable institutional framework for the development of the market. Moreover, institutions will facilitate trade and investment with the West due to their similarity to western laws and institutions. The pursuit of this strategy has led to some seemingly bizarre results. For example, the organization and high level of computerization envisioned in the legal framework creating a stock exchange in Poland ensure that it can handle a volume of transactions comparable to the United States stock exchanges; yet the number of shareholders and the volume of stock currently bought and sold in Poland are such that they could be quite adequately transacted and recorded by means of the bookkeeping technology of the Victorian era.

This dichotomy between the most up-to-date laws and institutions and the primitive state of the market has led some economists to argue for a more evolutionary approach. They point out that institutions arise and disappear in response to the specific needs of their environment. Under a given set of economic conditions, a given institution will arise if it can provide a useful service at minimal resource cost, and the same institution will be cast aside when its services either are no longer needed or are provided more cheaply by some other institution. Thus, for example, at some volume of stock trades, an informal system of curb brokers, such as the precursor of the New York Stock Exchange, may be most efficient, while only with a higher volume of trades do a formal stock exchange and computerization make economic sense. In a more general sense, since the Eastern European economies differ from those of the West in more fundamental ways, such as the level of development, the degree of privatization, the size distribution of firms, and the extent of foreign ownership, it is argued that a more evolutionary approach permitting institutions appropriate to this environment to arise and compete for survival would make greater sense than would the wholesale importing of western institutions.

The drafting of laws has been characterized by a similar debate. Some argue that foreign laws, often those of EC countries, should simply be translated and enacted *tout court*. The difficulty is that there are insufficient legal scholars to translate the necessary laws so that lawmakers are forced to draft their own instead. In any case, most laws are rather simple frameworks that must be filled in through the accumulation of precedents that arise as the courts apply the laws to concrete situations. This fact has led to efforts to revive the business codes existing in these countries during the inter-War period. The problem with this approach is that such codes are often outdated and thus do not apply to modern-day business practices or to modern technologies. Moreover, they differ from EC law and thus tend to create obstacles to trade between Eastern and Western Europe.

The Conceptual Issues of Privatization

Even more difficult from a conceptual point of view than the creation of markets is the privatization of state-owned property, which includes not only virtually all industrial enterprises, but also agricultural and urban land, as well as commercial and residential buildings.

Privatizing this property involves difficult tradeoffs between three desiderata: equity, efficiency, and practicality. An equitable distribution of property would be one that was fair to the residents of the country. One element of fairness is that owners of property seized by the Communist regime should be entitled to some form of restitution. While the notion of restitution seems quite reasonable, its implementation has been something of a political football. Thus, different types of property, e.g., large vs. small firms, agricultural vs. urban land, as well as different property owners, e.g., those who emigrated vs. those who did not, foreign vs. domestic, those whose property was seized after the Communist takeover vs. those whose property was seized beforehand, most notably Jews whose property was seized during the Nazi occupation, have been treated differently by the legislation on restitution. There is also the problem that simply returning specific pieces of property to owners after 40 years may either undercompensate them if, for example, their property has been run down, or overcompensate them if the state has made significant investments in the property over the past 40 years. In general, small shops and houses have been the easiest to return to former owners. Industrial property is more problematic and agricultural land is likely to be the thorniest issue of all.

Once restitution has been carried out, it then remains to put the rest of the assets to be privatized into the hands of the public in a way that is equitable. It is generally agreed that distributional equity in this case means allocation that gives each citizen a relatively equal share of the value of assets to be privatized. One immediate obstacle to this is that it is impossible to value the assets being privatized with any degree of accuracy. Each firm, of course, has a book value, but in the distorted economic systems of Eastern Europe, even more than in market economies, the book value has little to do with the economic value of an asset. Thus, any privatization scheme, other than the cumbersome one giving each citizen an identical portfolio of assets being privatized, stands the chance of being rejected on grounds of *ex ante* inequality. Worse, once markets are introduced, the economic, rather than bookkeeping, values of the privatized firms will reveal themselves as share prices of profit-making firms rise and those of unprofitable firms sink. The result may be an exceptionally rapid, and therefore socially and politically unacceptable, redistribution of wealth from one that was *ex ante* relatively egalitarian to one that has become, *ex post*, quite unequal.

A major objective of privatization is to improve the efficiency of the firms. Under state ownership, firms were neither subject to the threat of bankruptcy nor induced to maximize profits. Rather, their managers pursued policies that sought to extract financial resources from the owner, the state, in return for fostering social objectives, such as high levels of employment or exports or the production of desired products, all of which tended to interfere with profit maximization. Since private owners, unlike the state, do not have "deep pockets," privatized firms will face the threat of bankruptcy. Moreover, private owners can be expected to exercise greater control over managerial objectives and performance. The difficulty with this theory of corporate governance, as the extensive literature on the separation of ownership and management in the modern corporation teaches us, is that many owners, each with a relatively small stake in a corporation, have little incentive to monitor the behavior of managers and little possibility for mobilizing their fellow stockholders to take action to replace ineffective managers. Thus, what is required is some concentration of shares in the hands of one or more large shareholders to whom the benefits of monitoring managerial behavior exceed the costs and who can influence the selection of managers. Such a concentration of shares, however beneficial it may be from the standpoint of efficiency, of course is inconsistent with the broad and relatively egalitarian distribution of assets required by equity considerations. Moreover, large owners are also likely to attempt to utilize political pressure to protect their assets against the difficulties many firms will face during the transition process.

Finally, there are problems of timing. Privatization can come about partly from the bottom up, as small private businesses emerge and expand, but their ability to do so will surely depend on the existence of a "level playing field" between them and the large state-owned firms. Moreover, it will be a long time before such small businesses can grow to a size where they can take over large state-owned firms. Thus, it is the de-etatization of the existing industrial stock that will largely determine the pace of privatization. Therefore, putting the state-owned firms into private hands has to be done quickly, forcing a certain measure of arbitrariness and pragmatism into competition with the objectives of equity and efficiency.

Given these competing objectives, it is not surprising that a rather disparate set of alternative proposals for privatization has appeared. Among the most radical privatization proposals to come forward is the so-called voucher scheme, in which every citizen would be given vouchers with some nominal value attached to them to be used to bid for shares of the firms being privatized. The scheme could be modified so that risk-averse voucher holders could obtain either fixed-interest securities or shares of mutual funds that would use the vouchers of the participants to purchase shares of the firms. Moreover, foreign investors could be accommodated, either by allowing them to buy stock at some premium over the price paid by residents, or by allowing them to bid for vouchers offered either by the state or by the citizens of the country.

The voucher scheme is attractive primarily because it provides for a quick and extensive privatization of state property while simultaneously establishing at least the relative values of firms, an excellent starting point for the creation of a viable stock market. The proposal is also appealing in terms of *ex ante* equity, since everyone starts off with the same number of vouchers. *Ex post* equity is less of a problem since it depends largely on the choices made by each individual regarding the allocation of his or her vouchers. Nevertheless, given the lack of any useful information about the economic performance or prospects of the firms being privatized, it can be argued that citizens are being forced to determine their future wealth on the basis of little more than an arbitrary game of chance. Finally, the voucher scheme is appealing because it creates a broadly based "people's capitalism," so that, with everyone a shareholder, there should be strong political and social support for an economic system based on markets and private property.

The shortcomings of the voucher scheme are equally clear. First, the broad shareholding that it implies means that shareholder monitoring of managerial performance will be weak, and managers will tend to be unresponsive to the objectives of the owners. Second, the distribution of wealth to the population is seen by critics of the voucher scheme as being inflationary since, with greater wealth, people will wish to consume more.

A possible solution to the efficiency defects of the voucher scheme is to give the stock of the firms being privatized to holding companies, which would then be able to exercise effective oversight of managers. The public would receive shares in the holding companies. The use of holding companies also has serious shortcomings. It is possible that holding companies would collude with management of the firms they own, preferring to keep poorly performing firms afloat rather than making the difficult decision to close them down. Moreover, the power wielded by holding companies would be enormous and, in the end, the holding companies might well reproduce many of the shortcomings of the old Communist system, with state control practiced through the holding companies.

The alternative to the voucher scheme is a program of selling state-owned enterprises to the public. A state agency, possibly aided by foreign consultants and bankers, would establish a fair market value for state-owned firms and then sell its shares to the public, including possibly to foreigners. The principal advantages are that the scheme is non-inflationary and, indeed, raises revenue for the government, and that large stockholders are likely to emerge, promoting enterprise efficiency.

This approach has shortcomings in equity and practicality. If the shares are to be sold, then the wealthier members of society will emerge with the majority of the shares. Not only is this rather unegalitarian, it also favors those who had high incomes under the former Communist regime. Since these individuals were often part of the old political and economic power structure, the sale of state-owned firms is often referred to as the "embourgeoisment" of the "nomenclatura" (those appointed to high positions by the Communist party). Thus, the system not only fails to provide much equity, but appears to reward those who, to most people in Eastern Europe, least deserve it. A further problem is the role of foreigners who, because of the undervalued currencies of the Eastern European countries, and because of their access to international credit markets, can easily outspend the residents of these countries in bidding for firms being sold.

The scheme is also short on practicality. Firms put up for sale will be difficult to value, and the process of selling them will necessarily be time-consuming, meaning that privatization will be slow. In Hungary, the valuation of firms, especially those sold to foreigners, has become the object of bitter controversy, further slowing the process. The population of the Eastern European countries lack the liquid assets to buy shares in firms being privatized and, given the uncertain economic future of these countries, they seem disinclined to trade cash for risky shares.

The Conceptual Issues
of Macroeconomic Management

The change from plan to market also means that both the sources of government revenue and the size and nature of government expenditures must change. Under the old system, the principal sources of revenue were the turnover tax, a highly variegated set of levies on sales of consumer goods, and a set of levies on the assets and profits of enterprises. To move to a system of uniform sales or value-added taxes and of taxes on enterprise profits will, in a market environment, involve a good deal of uncertainty, not the least because neither consumption nor profits is likely to be predictable in a period of chaotic transformation. At the same time, a new system of income taxes must be introduced to equitably spread the tax burden to individuals who engage in private enterprise or who own large amounts of stock. What rates to set for these taxes, and what government revenues will be are difficult questions to answer given the lack of experience with a market economy.

There will be equal uncertainty on the expenditure side. While the state budget should no longer have to subsidize inefficient industries and the consumption of food and other consumer goods, new and more volatile claims on the government will appear. The creation and financing of a social safety net is critical, both to provide for those suffering from the new phenomenon of unemployment and to keep the incomes of pensioners and the poor from being overtaken by inflation.

In addition to uncertainties about the government's revenues and expenditures, policymakers will face uncertainty about the efficacy and impact of traditional tools of macroeconomic policy. Although changes in the money supply, interest rates, government expenditure and taxes, and the exchange rate will have some effect on aggregate economic activity, the magnitude of these effects cannot be predicted *ex ante*. In western economies, economists have had a long period of experience with these policy tools, which enables them to make some estimate of the impact of changes of policy on economic activity, although there is still considerable uncertainty and controversy about macroeconomic policy. This uncertainty will be considerably greater for Eastern European policymakers who must deal with much larger macroeconomic shocks using tools at whose precise effects they can only guess.

As these complex problems of transition and integration into the world economy are being worked out in the reforming countries, they have an impact on short-term economic developments and, simultaneously, the success of the transition measures is strongly affected by short-term economic developments. Thus, it is to the analysis of these short-term trends and their interaction with the transition measures that we now turn.

Macroeconomic Developments in Eastern Europe

In each of the three Eastern European countries undergoing the transition to capitalism, the transition measures have been to some extent limited by, but also have themselves strongly influenced, the macroeconomic environment.

Czechoslovakia

Of the three Eastern European countries undergoing transition, Czechoslovakia was the least prepared intellectually to undertake such a step. Few people within or outside the country anticipated the rapid collapse of the government that occurred in the winter of 1989. The economy, while lacking dynamism, at least was not in the state of crisis that characterized neighboring Poland, and the Communist party showed few signs of concern. Moreover, Czechoslovak economists had been unable to openly discuss measures for even modest reform, much less for the transition from communism to capitalism. The regime installed in the wake of the 1968 Warsaw Pact invasion of the country had purged many of the leading reform economists, consigning some of them to manual labor, and those who remained in the profession clearly understood that economic reform was a politically sensitive subject best avoided by economists.

It is thus understandable that 1990 was a year of slow groping toward an acceptable reform package. Early in the year, two competing packages were put forward, one popularly associated with Valtr Komarek, the popular head of the Forecasting Institute of the Academy of Sciences and Deputy Prime Minister in the government that took power in the wake of the "Velvet Revolution," the other with Vaclav Klaus, the articulate if acerbic Finance Minister and self-proclaimed disciple of Milton Friedman. The conservatives who sided with Komarek preferred a slow transition process where a period of some eight to ten years would be required to implement structural changes that would eventually permit the freeing of prices. In these proposals, there also was some searching for a "third way," some means of combining the social equity and egalitarianism of socialism with the efficiency of the market, in part reflecting the slogan of the reformers of 1968 who had sought to create "socialism with a human face." Privatization was also to proceed relatively slowly, with state-owned enterprises gradually being sold off to domestic or foreign buyers.

The more radical proposals called for a more rapid elimination of price subsidies and the freeing of prices within four to five years, a much more rapid privatization accelerated by the use of a voucher scheme and a sharp devaluation of the Czechoslovak koruna in order to set the stage for its convertibility.

During the first half of 1990, progress on resolving the conflict between the conservatives and the radical reformers moved slowly, in large part because the political situation was dominated by the Civic Forum, an umbrella organization for all the groups who had opposed the Communists. In such a heterodox amalgam of views, compromise rather than choice was preferable, and thus hard decisions were often difficult to reach. Moreover, until the June 1990 elections, the rump Parliament was loathe to take any important policy measures. Since the parliamentary elections and the split of the Civic Forum, with a group headed by President Havel favoring more gradual and measured reform and the remainder siding with Vaclav Klaus, the reform has begun to move forward along the agenda set out by the radicals.

In the summer of 1990, food and energy subsidies were eliminated, leading to a sharp jump of more than 25 percent in prices for these items. This tended to squeeze the profits of firms dependent on energy inputs, since their output prices remained frozen. A further price liberalization was introduced in January 1991, leading to another surge of inflation, with food prices increasing by 30 percent in three weeks. Because the government is pursuing a strongly anti-inflationary policy, it is hoped that these are one-time price jumps rather than the precursors of an inflationary spiral.

Privatization has also begun. Parliament passed a restitution law, which cleared the way for the so-called small privatization to begin. Under this program, retail and service establishments were auctioned off to the public. The auctions attracted a good deal of public interest and appear to have had the hoped-for result of improving the assortment and quality of service in these establishments. Large privatization, meaning privatization of large state-owned enterprises, will be carried out with the aid of a voucher scheme to promote a rapid and broad diffusion of ownership.

Finally, in 1991, the Czechoslovak koruna was made internally convertible at a rate of 28 koruna/$. The convertibility is somewhat limited in that Czechoslovak firms are required to turn their foreign exchange earnings in to the state bank, but it is a step toward the liberalization of the foreign trade regime.

The macroeconomic policy of the reforms has been as conservative as their transition program has been radical. This policy stance was dictated in part by the economic situation that the new regime inherited from the Communists: a relatively small overhang of money in the hands of the public, little external debt, and stable prices. These positive inheritances the reformers could not afford to squander, since public opinion was clearly resistant to the outbreak of inflation at a level such as in neighboring Poland, or to a level of foreign debt that existed in both Poland and Hungary. Thus, the government ran in 1990, and is hoping to run in 1991, a budget surplus. The money supply has also remained stagnant, resulting in the lackluster macroeconomic perfor-mance shown in Table 2.

Table 2
Macroeconomic Indicators for Czechoslovakia, 1989-1991

	Percent of Growth		
	1989	1990	1991
Net Material Product	0.7	-3.3	n.a.
Consumer Price Index	1.4	17.0	53.1
Employment	0.4	-2.7	n.a.
Nominal Wages	2.5	3.8	n.a.

SOURCE: Josef C. Brada, "The Economic Transition of Czechoslovakia From Plan to Market." *Journal of Economic Perspectives,* Vol. 5, No. 4 (Fall 1991).

With the government's economic policy locked into an anti-infla-tionary posture, the level of output and employment in Czechoslovakia has been determined largely by the effects of the transition and by exogenous events. One outcome of the price reforms has been to create large fluctuations in consumer demand. In 1990, consumer demand was strong, as people sought to stock up on goods in anticipation of the price increases scheduled for January 1991. Then in January, consumer demand collapsed, because of both higher prices and consumer satia-tion. With the government unable to intervene to stimulate demand, output, which had held relatively steady in 1990 thanks to the pur-chases of consumers, plunged and industrial production fell sharply, as Table 3 clearly shows. Moreover, inflation has increased and unem-ployment has started to become a serious problem, with the level of unemployment increasing from month to month as may be seen from Table 4.

Table 3
Monthly Industrial Production in Czechoslovakia, 1989-1991
(1989=100)

	J	F	M	A	M	J	J	A	S	O	N	D
1989	95	92	105	100	100	106	88	98	101	117	108	96
1990	93	89	100	100	99	98	85	93	94	115	106	89
1991	89	84	80	79								

SOURCE: Author's estimates from *Týdeník Hospodárských Novin,* May 23, 1991.

In addition to the collapse of consumer demand, the collapse of exports to the Soviet Union and the other Eastern European countries could not be offset completely by strong consumer demand in 1990 and not at all in 1991. The decline in Soviet demand for Czechoslovak exports was particularly serious in Slovakia, whose industries were heavily oriented toward the production of goods, including armaments, for the Soviet Union. The collapse of this trade has had a particularly severe impact on unemployment in Slovakia, exacerbating tense relations between Czechs and Slovaks.

Table 4
Monthly Increases in Unemployment in Czechoslovakia, 1990-1991
(In thousands)

	J	F	M	A	M	J	J	A	S	O	N	D
1990	-	-	-	7.4	8.8	12.6	19.4	27.4	43.9	57.3	67.2	77.0
1991	119.0	152.3	184.6	223.2	-	-	-	-	-	-	-	-

SOURCE: *Týdeník Hospodárských Novin*, May 23, 1991.

It is, of course, too early to tell whether the economy can recover from the decline in output and the rapid increase in prices. Public opinion polls and government statements both suggest that the country is bracing for difficult times ahead. With macroeconomic policy locked into a deflationary stance, there are few ways in which output growth can be generated through increased demand.

Hungary

Unlike Czechoslovakia, which had much to do to catch up with thinking about transformation and reform, Hungary was the leader of Eastern Europe both in the theory and application of the market to a socialist economy. However, hampered by both the caution of domestic politicians and the limits to reform implicitly imposed by the Soviet Union, Hungary's road to the market, begun in 1968 with the introduction of the New Economic Mechanism (NEM), has been a slow and tortuous one.

On the positive side, relative prices were less distorted than in other Eastern European countries, the role of small-scale private enterprise in services and in industry was quite large, and the Hungarian economics profession was made up of a large number of well-trained individuals who were familiar with western economic theory and who had regular contacts with western economists.

On the other side of the ledger, the greater sophistication of Hungarian bankers and economists did not help them to avoid incurring a foreign debt of over $20 billion, larger on a *per capita* basis than that of Poland. As a result, for the past 10 years, Hungary has had to follow a deflationary policy of limiting investment and output growth so as to restrain the demand for hard-currency imports. This led to a long-term stagnation of living standards and the servicing of Hungary's foreign debt has thus assumed such overwhelming importance that it virtually dictates macroeconomic policy.

Hungary has been following a policy of gradual and slow price adjustments and liberalizations since the introduction of the NEM in 1968. Since price liberalizations generally mean price increases, the government has sought to offset the effects of inflation on poor people and pensioners by simultaneously raising minimum wages and pensions, although this policy is constrained by the need to keep aggregate demand in check. Moreover, despite the long record of price liberalization, the reformers have faced seriously distorted energy and raw materials prices as well as distortions in rents, some food prices, and a patchwork of firm-specific taxes and subsidies that hamper rational economic calculation. The Antal government has not had great success in attacking these distortions, its most humiliating setback occurring when a protest by Budapest taxi drivers forced the cancellation of a 60 percent increase in gasoline prices.

Small privatization is well-advanced in Hungary, with private restaurants and retail outlets having been permitted for many years. More recently, private small-scale provision of services and even the manufacture of goods was permitted. Big privatization, the de-etatization of Hungary's large state-owned enterprises, is proceeding more slowly, reflecting the philosophy of the ruling Democratic Forum party. Privatization of large state-owned enterprises was allowed by the Transformation and Corporation Laws, which set out the terms under which a state-owned enterprise could be converted to a corporation whose stock would then be sold to domestic or foreign investors. This proved to be a most controversial measure leading to public outcry and scandal. In some cases, managers and workers were alleged to have sold enterprises to themselves at artificially low prices; in other cases, managers allegedly sold their firms to foreigners at low prices in order to ensure their, and their workers', job security. A State Property Agency was organized in early 1990 to regulate privatization and to eliminate abuses of the Transformation Act. However, its head resigned shortly after taking office as the result of controversy over the privatization of Ibusz, the state travel agency, whose shares were quoted on the Vienna stock exchange at a premium of 200 percent over their original offer price. The Property Agency plans an orderly sale of enterprises, but the pace envisioned is so slow that, for the next 10 years or so, the bulk of large enterprises will remain in state hands. Since the more viable firms will be sold first, the state will increasingly come to hold Hungary's industrial cripples, and whether the government budget can stand the fiscal drain and the political system the pressure that workers in these industries will exert remains to be seen.

The macroeconomic performance of the Hungarian economy reflects the dilemmas and vacillation of the government. The level of output continues to decline, especially in industry, and so does industrial employment, as the figures in Table 5 indicate. To some extent in Hungary, as in the other two countries, these figures must be interpreted with some care. The existing statistical systems were conceived for a Communist economy where virtually all industrial activity took place in a relatively small number of large enterprises, and the reporting and compiling of production data for new, small private and cooperative businesses are in their infancy. Some estimate of the magnitude of this reporting gap in the case of Hungary can be gleaned from Note a in Table 5, which indicates how industrial production would have looked in 1990 had small businesses been more fully included in the measure of industrial output.

Table 5
Macroeconomic Indicators for Hungary, 1988-1991
(Previous year or corresponding period of previous year = 100)

	1988	1989	1990	1991
Industrial production	100.0	99.0	91.5[a]	86.7 (J-A)
Industrial employment	97.4	98.3	90.9	88.4 (J-A)
Consumer Price Index	115.5	117.0	128.9	107.5[b] 104.9[b] 103.7[b] 102.4[b]
Average gross wage in industry (ft)			13.397.0	15.230.0 (J-A)

SOURCE: Központi Statisztikai Hivatal, *Statisztikai Havi Közléyek*, Budapest, 1991.
a. Previous quarter = 100.
b. Previous month = 100.

While industrial output is falling, inflation continues apace, creating a dilemma for the government. In 1990, the Antal government introduced a strict monetarist policy, which reduced bank lending to enterprises and slowed money growth. Nevertheless, inflation in 1990 was nearly 30 percent and the further elimination of subsidies planned for 1991 led most Hungarian economists to predict a rate of inflation between 30 and 40 percent for that year. The government, however, abandoned its tight monetary policy in early 1991 in an effort to stimulate production, particularly in the export sector and among the more profitable firms. Despite this reversal of tight money policies, inflation in 1991 appears to be abating. At the same time, neither unemployment nor industrial production are showing signs of recovery. Thus, the government, because of an inability to gauge the impact of policy measures and the lag with which they affect the economy, is forced to choose between two options. One is to assume that tight monetary policy is ineffective and to opt for easy money with the potential danger of inflation and the potential gain of higher employment and output. Alternatively, current developments can be interpreted as showing that monetary policy can, with a certain lag, fight inflation and that some monetary restraint ought therefore to be retained while waiting for the positive effects of the relaxation of the ultra-tight money policy of 1990 on production in the second half of 1991.

How much of the fall in industrial production in Hungary is due to domestic policies and how much to external events is difficult to judge, although it would seem reasonable to assign much of the blame to the collapse of trade with the USSR and with the other socialist countries. This decline in trade has been particularly large and difficult to adjust to for Hungarian heavy industry. The curtailment of credit by Hungarian banks, on the other hand, as in Czechoslovakia, has been a source of worry for managers. To a large extent, however, the worst effects of this policy on production have been mitigated by the expedience of firms delaying payments to their suppliers. While the long-term effects of such an expansion of interfirm credit can be catastrophic, such credits do not appear to be the source of the current problems of Hungarian industry.

There are also some bright signs in the Hungarian economy. The private sector has been relatively dynamic, with a rapid growth of output and employment that has as yet eluded official statistics. Moreover, unless Hungarian agriculture suffers either from excessive organizational change or a lack of industrial inputs, it too is capable of making a positive contribution to the growth of output and exports. Finally, Hungary has been especially successful in attracting major foreign investors: General Electric has purchased Tungsram, Hungary's light bulb manufacturer; General Motors has invested in the huge Raba factory; and other western investors are participating in Hungarian banking, electronics, and telecommunications. Nevertheless, the slide in domestic output must be arrested and, since the economy is likely to suffer shocks to aggregate demand as trade with the USSR continues to decline, the only means of reflating the economy appears to be a rapid reorientation of trade toward the West or a domestic reflation spearheaded by foreign investment and consumer demand.

Poland

Poland is unique among the Eastern European countries in two ways. First, it entered upon its reform with a government that was perceived to be in a strong position to bring about a radical reform because it had a mandate from the population to bring about order out of economic chaos. This mandate was based on the face that, prior to 1990, the economy had been operating on a self-sustaining inflationary spiral. Due to low consumer prices, the government had to subsidize production, which led to a large government deficit. This deficit was covered by printing money, leading to higher wages and costs, necessitating higher subsidies for producers, and setting off another round of the spiral. As Table 6 indicates, in 1989, inflation was high by any standard, but sales, and therefore production, increased very little, with most of the increase in sales coming in anticipation of the freeing of prices in 1990.

Table 6
Macroeconomic Indicators for Poland, 1988-1991
(Previous year or corresponding period in previous year= 100)

	1989	1990	1991
Average employment	98.0	91.1	90.6 (J-M)
Average monthly wage	391.8	498.0	113.4[a] (J-M)
Consumer Price Index	351.1	684.7	112.7[b] 106.7[b] 104.5[b] 102.7[b] 102.7[b]
Real retail trade	109.0	74.9	70.3[b] 102.1[b] 106.0[b] 120.0[b]

SOURCE: Glowny Urzad Statystyczny, *Biuletin Statystyczny*, Warzawa, 1991.
a. Previous quarter = 100.
b. Previous month = 100.

This strong mandate and a perilous economic situation enabled the government to introduce a unique and radical freeing of prices in January 1990 that is popularly called the "big bang." Developed by the Deputy Prime Minister, L. Balcerowicz, the program freed prices while introducing strict controls over nominal wages. In view of the artificially low prices that had existed and of the huge overhang of unspent money in the hands of the population, prices of consumer goods almost doubled in January, but then inflation subsided to a rate of 5-10 percent per month, thus ending the hyperinflationary spiral.

This increase in prices, coupled with wage restraint, reduced both real incomes and private wealth held in the form of cash. As a result, consumer demand declined by over 20 percent. Polish firms responded to this decline in demand first by continuing production, some of which was used to rebuild stocks that had been exhausted by the buying splurge that occurred just prior to the freeing of prices. However, production for inventories could not continue forever and, with sales remaining at low levels, firms began to reduce production and to lay off workers. Table 7 shows the monthly evolution of unemployment in Poland, which continues to increase. Like Hungary, Poland has reached a point in the decline of output where some domestic or foreign source of reflation must be found to build on the positive results of the "big bang."

Table 7
Evolution of Unemployment in Poland, 1990-1991
(Percent of economically active population unemployed)

	J	F	M	A	M	J	J	A	S	O	N	D
1990	0.3	0.8	1.5	1.9	2.4	3.1	3.8	4.5	5.0	5.5	5.9	6.1
1991	6.5	6.8	7.1	7.3	7.7	8.5	-	-	-	-	-	-

SOURCE: Glowny Urzad Statystyczny, *Biuletin Statystyczny,* Warszawa, 1991.

Among these positive results is the ending of high rates of inflation; indeed, as Table 6 indicated, the rate of inflation appears to be abating significantly in 1991. The creation of a rational price system in Poland is a further benefit, although it has not yet been fully utilized to guide a restructuring of Polish industry. Finally, the Polish zloty was made convertible at 9,500 zloty/$, and it has depreciated only slightly since January 1990. The cost of these gains in terms of lower living standards, unemployment and foregone production are, of course, quite high, and the defeat of the Mazowiecky government at the polls by Lech Walesa may reflect society's evaluation of these gains and losses, although Balcerowicz, the architect of the "big bang," has retained control over economic policy.

While the Polish government has acted to create markets in a radical and seemingly quite effective way, there has been much less progress on privatization. The broad outlines of the process are clear, but the final enabling legislation is not as yet in place. The Polish procedure is to mix equity with efficiency by combining sales of shares for cash with a voucher scheme. When a firm is privatized, the bulk of the shares will be sold, some to the public and a "core owner" who will own a large enough bloc to induce efficient monitoring of managers. Another bloc of shares, about 20 percent of the total, will be offered to the workers at preferential rates, and the remainder of the shares will be divided between the government and the Polish population, who will be given vouchers with which to obtain such shares. The strength of the procedure is that it provides for a broad and relatively egalitarian distribution of some of the stock of privatized firms with the concentration of shareholding needed for efficiency. The disadvantages are, first, the complexity of the scheme, which means that privatization will be a drawn-out process, and second, the coexistence of a variety of shareholders who acquire their shares under different conditions and with possibly quite different objectives.

Conclusions

In all three countries, the principal objective factors leading to the decline in economic activity are the collapse of trade with the USSR and the effects of anticipated price changes on consumption. While there is little that governments in the region could do to avoid these shocks, the decline in production in the region has somewhat mistakenly been attributed to the process of economic reform. The major economic danger facing Eastern Europe is that this mistake will lead policymakers to behave as if such declines are an inevitable aspect of reform and to delay the reflation of their economies, thus drawing out the hardships faced by the populations of the region and undermining popular support for the transformation to capitalism.

Integrating Eastern Europe into the World Economy

Sources of Pressure for Greater East-West Trade

The countries of Eastern Europe are being pushed and pulled into integrating themselves more closely into the international system of trade and finance. This is good news since, in the long run, such inte-

gration will stimulate investment, rationalize these countries' economies, and foster technological progress. However, in the short run, the
forced pace of integration is likely to prove costly as many painful
readjustments will have to be made.

The push for increasing economic relations with the West comes
largely from the disappearance of the Council for Mutual Economic
Assistance (CMEA), which promoted trade among the socialist countries, and from the collapse of the Soviet Union, above all, and of the
other economies of the region. The CMEA mechanism had maintained
a high level of trade among the Eastern European economies and
between them and the USSR. It maintained this high level of trade by
means of mechanisms that facilitated trade among nonmarket economies, including a system of trade agreements that enabled CMEA
members to negotiate exchanges of goods among themselves and an
international payment system based on the transferable ruble. While
this system had its shortcomings, and was quite cumbersome when
compared to western trading arrangements such as the EC, it did facilitate trade among these countries, even if its promotion of intermember
trade was based in part on the diversion of Eastern European trade
away from the West.

The CMEA mechanism no longer exists, in part due to the abolition
of planning in the reforming Eastern European countries, which makes
the government-negotiated trade agreements irrelevant. Moreover, in
1990, the members of CMEA agreed that, from 1991 on, intra-CMEA
trade would take place at world market prices rather than at prices
negotiated bilaterally among members, and that trade transactions
would be paid for in dollars and not by means of the CMEA's transferable ruble. Thus, the two integrating mechanisms that bound the
region's economies together, trade agreements and the transferable
ruble system of clearing trade, were eliminated, and no new measures
to maintain the level of intraregional trade have been brought forward
to replace them.

In addition to the collapse of the CMEA, economic problems within
the CMEA member countries have acted to reduce the volume of
intraregional trade. The most important factor has been the economic

collapse of the USSR. The Soviet Union is the largest trading partner for each of the Eastern European countries, exporting fuels and raw materials to them in return for machinery and consumer manufactures. Due to declining Soviet oil production and the Soviet need to divert oil exports to the West to repay debts and to pay for western goods, Soviet oil deliveries to Eastern Europe fell by some 20 percent in 1990 and will fall again, possibly by even more, in 1991. Moreover, the Soviet Union reformed its trading system, decentralizing foreign trade decisions to individual firms, but these firms have no means of obtaining the currency needed to import from Eastern Europe. Thus, many large enterprises in Eastern Europe found themselves in a very difficult situation. Their supplies of energy and raw materials from the USSR were disappearing and Soviet customers, who had accounted for the bulk if not all of the output of these firms, were unable to purchase any goods.

In 1990, trade with other CMEA countries and with the USSR was further hampered by the realization that outstanding debts in transferable rubles would have to be repaid, after 1990, in convertible currencies. Thus, some countries were eager to export, but not to import, in order to build transferable ruble claims against their neighbors, and subsequently to convert these into claims payable in hard currencies. Of course, with all the Eastern European countries seeking to increase exports to each other and simultaneously to decrease imports from each other, the result was a decline in intra-Eastern European trade. The Soviet Union continued to be wiling to import for transferable rubles, but its Eastern European partners did not want to accumulate large ruble claims against the USSR, fearing that both the difficulties faced by the USSR in paying western exporters and the political instability of the country would make eventual repayment of these claims highly uncertain. Thus, they unilaterally acted to reduce their exports to the USSR. Finally, the unification of Germany eliminated the German Democratic Republic from intra-CMEA trade, a process that began well before unification took place as East German firms canceled trade contracts for imports, realizing that they needed to husband their money for the difficult period they would face after unification.

The net effect of these forces is amply revealed by Table 8, which shows Polish trade cleared in transferable rubles and in dollars. The decline in ruble trade reflects both the physical decline in the volume of intraregional trade and its conversion from ruble to dollar clearing. Similarly, the expansion of dollar trade reflects both the increased volume of trade with the West and the greater use of hard currencies in intraregional trade. Despite the redirection of trade toward the West, the total trade of each of the countries of Eastern Europe has declined sharply in the past two years, with obvious effects on production and employment in the traditional export countries.

Table 8
Polish Trade by Currency of Settlement, 1989-1991
(Previous year or corresponding period of previous year = 100)

	Exports settled in:		Imports settled in:	
	Transferable rubles	Convertible currencies	Transferable rubles	Convertible currencies
1989	102.3	102.7	93.4	106.3
1990	90.1	140.9	65.7	106.3
1991-J	29.1	168.7	30.1	194.2
-F	27.9	130.2	40.8	163.3
-M	11.7	108.2	26.0	227.7
-A	23.0	122.3	15.5	301.0
-M	19.6	135.5	6.2	200.3
-J	11.6	125.7	11.2	139.2

SOURCE: Glowny Urzad Statystyczny, *Biuletin Statystyczny,* Warszawa, 1991.

While the collapse of intraregional trade has sent Czechoslovakia, Hungary, and Poland searching for new markets in the West, such a westward turn has other, more positive motivation as well. The Eastern Europeans realize that much of their industrial technology and equipment is obsolete. Thus, they view trade with the West as indispensable to raising the productivity and competitiveness of their economies and ultimately to improving their living standards. Moreover, the Eastern Europeans believe that they must act quickly to become an integral element of the western economic system or they may lose their chance, if not forever, then for a long time. The closer integration of the European Community, scheduled for 1992, has had a powerful impact on Eastern Europe because Eastern Europeans want to become part of the EC. They see themselves as sharing a common cultural heritage with the peoples of the EC, and they are caught up with the "Euro-optimism" that the 1992 program has engendered. At the same time, they believe that, as the forces let loose by EC-92 begin to integrate Western Europe more closely, it will become increasingly difficult for other countries to join. Thus, they believe that there is a narrow window of opportunity in which they must forge the economic links to the EC that will be the precursors to admission to full membership.

The Magnitude of the Restructuring of Eastern Europe's Trade

To understand what the difficulties of redirecting Eastern Europe's trade toward the West will be, we first must obtain a rough estimate of the volume and composition of the trade that is likely to be directed toward western markets. The CMEA accounted for about 8 percent of world trade. However, some 55 percent of the trade of the CMEA countries, or some 4 percent of world trade, was with each other. Due to the effects of CMEA integration, intraregional trade was some two to three times as high as it would have been had these countries not belonged to CMEA. Thus, the demise of the CMEA should reduce intraregional trade by about one-half, a volume of trade equal to slightly more than 2 percent of world trade. While the CMEA promoted intraregional trade, the total trade of its members was not excessively high, and it may be assumed that economic rationality would dictate that, rather than having their trade volume fall by 25 percent as the result of the demise of the CMEA, Eastern European countries would prefer to retain their present level of trade by redirecting transactions to the world market.

Thus, the first question is whether the redirection of goods equal to 2 percent of the world's international trade toward the world market would be feasible. Since world trade grew by 6-8 percent per year in the 1980s, it would seem that a further increase of 2 percent, especially if phased in over three to four years, would present few problems for international markets. However, once one moves beyond the aggregate and examines the commodity composition of the trade likely to be redirected, the problem appears to be more serious. Eastern Europe's exports to the USSR consisted largely of machinery and equipment. It is these export capacities in heavy industry that will have to seek new outlets in the West. At the same time, Eastern European imports from the USSR consisted to a large extent of fuels and raw materials, often at artificially low prices. When one examines the existing exports of Eastern Europe to the West, it quickly becomes evident that they consist largely of semi-fabricates and partially processed goods, not the machinery and equipment whose quality and technological levels, while suitable for the Soviet market, are unacceptable in the West. At the same time, imports of fuels and raw materials at world market prices will present a major inflationary shock for Eastern Europe.

The lack of competitiveness of Eastern European heavy industry on world markets means that policymakers in these countries face two choices. One of these is to attempt to make their heavy industry competitive on world markets by importing western technology, equipment and technical and business know-how. This, however, would be a vast undertaking, could proceed only slowly, and, most likely, could be achieved only by granting a good deal of influence to foreign firms and expanding foreign direct investment. Such a strategy may face political resistance from populations unused to foreign owners and to being buffeted by the impersonal workings of the world markets.

The other way of expanding exports to the West would be to expand those industries whose products Eastern Europe has been able to sell on world markets. The difficulty with this strategy is that such products come primarily from low-wage, low-skill, and low-technology industries. To expand such industries would be costly in terms of the costs of moving labor and capital from other sectors, and it would be unpopular because it neither accords with people's expectations regarding progress nor provides for the type of high-wage employment that is available in heavy industry. Moreover, it is precisely agricultural and low-wage industrial products that face the greatest protectionist barriers on western markets.

Thus, the redirection of trade is likely to entail significant short-term costs in terms of unemployment, the shutting down of uncompetitive industries, and the need to devalue currencies to make Eastern European products competitive on western markets. The investment climate in the region will be a major determinant of how much western investment will be willing to undertake the rehabilitation of the region's industrial structure.

Conclusions

This essay has stressed the interaction of short- and long-term forces on the economic performance of Eastern Europe. While the catalog of problems and challenges facing the region seems, and indeed is, daunting, there are also positive elements at work. The populations of these countries are reasonably well educated and cultural levels are relatively high. People are hopeful of a better future, suggesting that they will respond to economic incentives. The most important issue for economic policymaking is that policymakers are able to understand the disparate forces acting on the region and frame the correct policy responses. Without a sound policy framework, the challenges facing the region surely cannot be overcome.

INDEX